Arden Perfori

CW00539435

Shakespeare and Meisner

Arden Performance Companions

Shakespeare and Meisner

A Practical Guide for Actors, Directors, Students and Teachers

Aileen Gonsalves and Tracy Irish

THE ARDEN SHAKESPEARE
LONDON • NEW YORK • OXFORD • NEW DELHI • SYDNEY

THE ARDEN SHAKESPEARE
Bloomsbury Publishing Plc
50 Bedford Square, London, WC1B 3DP, UK
1385 Broadway, New York, NY 10018, USA
29 Earlsfort Terrace, Dublin 2, Ireland

BLOOMSBURY, THE ARDEN SHAKESPEARE and the Arden Shakespeare logo
are trademarks of Bloomsbury Publishing Plc

First published in Great Britain 2021

Series design by Charlotte Daniels
Cover image © Getty Images

A catalogue record for this book is available from the British Library.

A catalog record for this book is available from the Library of Congress.

ISBN: HB: 978-1-3501-1840-9
       PB: 978-1-3501-1839-3
       ePDF: 978-1-3501-1841-6
       eBook: 978-1-3501-1842-3

Series: Arden Performance Companions

Typeset by RefineCatch Limited, Bungay, Suffolk
Printed and bound in Great Britain

To find out more about our authors and books visit www.bloomsbury.com
and sign up for our newsletters.

CONTENTS

Part Three Aileen Gonsalves in conversation with Tracy Irish about how Butterfly Theatre Company use Meisner's techniques

SERIES PREFACE

The Arden Performance Companions offer practice-focused introductions to different aspects of staging Shakespeare's plays: whether accounts of how Shakespearean drama may respond to particular systems of rehearsal and preparation, guides to how today's actors can understand and use different facets of Shakespeare's verbal style, or explorations of how particular modern practitioners have used Shakespeare's scripts as starting points for their own embodied thinking about the social and aesthetic possibilities of popular theatre.

The premise of this series is that the interpretation of Shakespeare is not confined to the literary analysis of his scripts, but also includes their rehearsal and performance. With this in mind, the Arden list of editions of Shakespeare expanded in 2017 to include not only heavily-annotated scholarly texts of each play, designed primarily for use in colleges and universities, but a new series, the Arden Performance Editions of Shakespeare, designed primarily for use in rehearsal rooms and at drama schools. Just as academic editions of Shakespeare may be supplemented by books introducing students to different modes of academic criticism, so these Arden Performance Companions seek to supplement the Arden Performance Editions, offering a rich variety of practical guidance on how Shakespeare's plays can be brought to life in contemporary performance.

AUTHORS' PREFACE

Aileen

I first saw Meisner actors doing his famous word repetition exercise in a damp basement workspace underneath the Troubadour restaurant in London twenty years ago. Their only text was, 'You're blinking / I'm blinking'. Suddenly I witnessed authentic connection moment to moment between two actors using irrelevant phrases, and have spent the intervening years in the glorious challenge of bringing that magic to some of the greatest text ever written. When I discovered Meisner, I found tremendous freedom – freedom from the insistent thinking, criticizing, second-guessing, constant monitoring and double-checking that was happening in my head whenever I took on a role. My excellent training at the Royal Central School of Speech and Drama had equipped me with a 'tool box' of approaches, but I was always in my head thinking very hard about which tool to use. In the deceptively simple exercise of Repetition, I saw the immediacy of connection to the other actor; the responsiveness and playfulness of actors having their attention not on themselves or even on what they were saying, but on each other. I realised the acting I had been taught, saw all around me, and was doing myself, was often superficial, polite and habitual. No one thought it was bad. It was all we knew. Now, I had seen something else, something vital that made me feel emotion. I realized the audience would only feel emotion if the feeling was *real*. Not acted or crafted beautifully, but actually *really felt* by the actor in that moment. Watching Repetition, I saw a way for authentic emotion to be truly felt in a moment and then let go in the next moment.

Tracy

I first met Aileen when we were both working at the RSC in 2008, but it was when we co-led a project in Oman for the World Shakespeare Festival in 2012 that we really discovered our common values and interests in working with Shakespeare. At that time I had barely heard of Meisner, but through Aileen's enthusiastic passion and her infectiously generous approach in leading Butterfly theatre company and her actor training courses, I learned rapidly. I quickly felt part of the Butterfly family – a large collective of not only talented, but warm, funny, witty individuals who have defined for me what an ensemble can be. My main interests are in how Shakespeare's language works in active communication and how theatre practice can help us to engage critically and creatively with the social world we live in. What I found in Meisner was an approach to acting that, although superficially contradictory to the valuing of words, felt instinctively complementary. The more we worked together and talked about our work, the more I found Meisner to be a very human process that can ground the language of Shakespeare in the actor's body without diminishing its power.

A sign on the wall of Meisner's classroom read 'An Ounce of BEHAVIOR is Worth a Pound of WORDS' (Meisner and Longwell 1987: 4). The unpicking of the relative valuing of behaviour and words when working with Shakespeare has been at the centre of many of the various discussions we have had in writing this book together. Together we have learned even more about the potential of what a partnership of Meisner and Shakespeare can offer, and we welcome you on that journey.

FOREWORD

Scott Williams

Sandy Meisner didn't do praise.

At least not in my experience. Classes at the Neighborhood Playhouse School of the Theatre, where I studied with him in the 1970s, were fascinating but often sepulchral affairs, filled with tension and fear and the wait for someone or other to be pulled up and thrown unceremoniously out of the room. So, when he doled out one of his considered nods and gave you a slight shrug denoting 'not bad', you left the classroom on a cloud, sure that you were the next Robert Duvall or Diane Keaton (heroes of ours, because they'd clearly survived before us the rigours of the Meisner experience).

I recall vowing privately in those faraway days that if I ever found myself in a teaching position – as I have for the more than forty years since – I would attempt a more uplifting environment in which to work.

So it gives me more than the usual pleasure to sing out the praises of Aileen Gonsalves and Tracy Irish, who have found an excitement and passion in the uses of Meisner's work, and who have squeezed all their enthusiasm into the pages you're about to read.

Aileen Gonsalves has been a treasured associate of mine for more than twenty years now, and has filled her work with a gusto and exhilaration which would have flattened Meisner. It is her extraordinary achievement that she has grasped the techniques that Meisner espoused and deeply investigated them in her rigorous and continuing exploration of the theatrical event.

Tracy Irish is a newer colleague, and one whose work with Aileen in these pages marks her as an equal partner in passion and in the pursuit of excellence in performance.

Together, these fine intellects have absorbed the exquisite concepts that Meisner so brilliantly (if astringently) taught, and focused their considerable insight on the greatest writing in the English language.

The irony here is that Meisner, in my experience, didn't have a lot to say about Shakespeare, and what he did have to say about British actors isn't appropriate to repeat in a family-oriented book. He was part of a generation of teachers, along with Strasberg, Adler, Kazan and the like, who were on a self-appointed mission to stamp out what they perceived as falsity in performance. The old terms, tossed about so liberally by them that their meaning is now slightly obscured, were 'presentational' and 'representational' acting – the first being deemed by Stanislavsky and others as the outward portrayal of an inner state (and therefore filled with intellectuality and untruth), and the latter standing in for the embodiment of an emotional state in which an actor undertakes to live out the life of the character with – and here's the key concept – moment-by-moment truthfulness.

Meisner thought Laurence Olivier, to take an example, didn't have a lot of truth in him. But I feel reasonably certain that he would have adored – no, strike that: he'd have given a grudging gesture of approval to today's British actors, who are so brilliant at combining the technical proficiency of their forebears with the quicksilver emotional aliveness of the best of the American actors.

Peter Brook has noted that each succeeding generation tests its best ideas about performance on Shakespeare. We see that truism abundantly played out in the successes of David Garrick and Edmund Kean, of Ellen Terry and Ira Aldridge, of Kathryn Hunter and Mark Rylance. All of these astonishing actors, and a great many more, test their mettle against Shylock and Viola and Dogberry and Timon and Lady Macbeth and, yes, Hamlet and Lear. They all live in their own age of performance, and yet thrill equally to the words put down more than 400 years ago which are as alive today as they were when flowing from Shakespeare's quill.

What this book does, and does to a fare-thee-well, is to offer insight, ideas and inspiration to twenty-first century actors as they approach Shakespeare, never denying Sanford Meisner's notions of 'truth' but equally honouring William Shakespeare's astonishing understanding of the human experience.

That's a remarkable achievement. One upon which even Meisner might have bestowed a smile.

ACKNOWLEDGEMENTS

We would like to thank our editors for all their help and advice: Abigail Rokison-Woodall, Michael Dobson, Simon Russell Beale, Meredith Benson and Margaret Bartley. Many thanks also to our interviewees: Scott Williams, Mike Bernardin, Amanda Ryan, Darren Raymond and Butterfly artists: Elle De Burgh, Caroline Colomei, Hayley Cusick, Nicholas Humphries, Charis King, Carla-Marie Metcalfe, Jen McGregor, Mathew McPherson, Sophie Rickman, Elliot Thomas and Oliver Towse. These interviews were carried out in late 2019 and early 2020, and we are immensely grateful for their time in talking to us and for their words, which have so enriched this book. We would like to thank all the staff and students we have worked with over the years at ArtsEd, RADA, Mountview, Rose Bruford, Drama Studio London, London College of Music, Edinburgh Acting School, Identity, ICAT, ISTA, Fourth Monkey, Film Club, University of Birmingham, University of West London, University of Heidelberg, University of Warwick, RSC, Inter-mission Youth Theatre, Horace Mann School and many other schools in the UK and internationally. Enormous thanks to the many, many brilliantly creative people we have worked with who have influenced and inspired us, particularly past and present members of Butterfly Theatre Company and the RSC, especially Cicely Berry. Lastly we would like to thank our friends and families for their unconditional patience and support, most notably Milo and Wilf Allegretti and Dominic Giles.

1

Introduction

Acting is not talking. It is living off the other fellow.
SANFORD MEISNER (1987: 42)

Sanford Meisner's name is now synonymous with an approach to acting that requires the truthful response of an actor bringing their own life to bear on inhabiting a text. He described his technique as 'in a nutshell ... the process of filling a cold text with your life' (1987: 169). He was one of the founding members of the Group Theatre in New York in the 1920s, along with Stella Adler, Lee Strasberg and Harold Clurman. The Group (described more fully in Chapter 2) were passionate young theatre makers, highly influenced by European developments in theatre, most especially through the work of Konstantin Stanislavsky. They challenged the status quo and their explorations developed into the various approaches characterized as Method Acting, all of which seek to make acting less about artifice and more about genuine emotional engagement. Meisner's own key development was to focus on what happens *between* actors. The acting approaches he developed have been taken forward by many teachers in their own ways, but the sense of an actor bringing a truthful, personal response to their work, which is *dependent* on the other actor, is the core of any Meisner approach.

For Meisner (1987: 15), acting is 'living truthfully under a given set of circumstances' with those circumstances defined by the director's interpretation of a playwright's words. He developed exercises to support an actor in finding ways to live truthfully, the most well-known of which is **Repetition**. Repetition is so called because the words the actors speak aloud express an observation made by one actor about the other, which their partner then repeats from their own perspective, for example, 'You're smiling', 'I'm smiling'. The phrase is repeated until something happens to make one of the actors change the words to another observation, perhaps, 'You moved your hand', 'I moved my hand'. This deceptively simple activity removes any need for either actor to 'act' – consciously creating a performance by improvising the speech and behaviour they *think* their character would use in that moment – and instead to respond instinctively in the moment. With Repetition, the actor has a simple phrase to say and does not need to 'go into their heads' to search for other words that are clever or witty or 'in character'. Instead, they focus on their partner and respond to how their partner makes them feel through their voice and behaviour as they open and close their mouths around whatever phrase it is they are repeating. The words in Repetition are unimportant – you may, for example, still be repeating 'You're smiling' when the smile has fallen away. Rather than having their attention on the words, Meisner wanted his actors to develop awareness of the emotional response expressed through those words and the close connection that this creates.

Meisner's technique, as it has been variously adopted and adapted, focuses on three sequential exercises: **Repetition, Independent Activity, Knock on the Door**; and the key concepts of **Preparation** and **As Ifs**. His inspiration came from the Group Theatre's explorations into Stanislavsky's legacy; however, these particular exercises, the rationale behind them and the supporting work with Preparation and As Ifs, can be regarded as created by Meisner and are specific to his technique. These activities are what Scott Williams, taught by Meisner himself, describes as 'the full work out for developing the actor'. Like an athlete using weights in the gym or a pianist doing scales, they are about the rigorous training of mind and muscle to respond unconsciously in the moment as the foundation that allows artistry to flourish freely.

The two key 'muscles' that Meisner's technique trains are: **seeing clearly** and **responding honestly from your point of view**. One of Meisner's basic principles is: 'What you do doesn't depend on you; it depends on the other fellow' (1987: 34). This means you need to see clearly how 'the other fellow' is behaving – not how you think the other fellow as a character should behave, but your personal perception of how that fellow human is actually behaving in that moment. Another of Meisner's basic principles is: 'Don't do anything unless something happens to make you do it' (1987: 34). This means allowing yourself to be affected by what you see clearly in the other fellow and then responding honestly from your point of view. The principle is most simply illustrated in Meisner's concept of pinch and ouch, where someone genuinely saying 'ouch' is justified by actually being pinched, not any pretence of pinching or ouching. Although Meisner uses this as a literal example, his point is to underline the metaphor of pinch and ouch: if you see clearly the 'pinch' of someone threatening you, your 'ouch' might be a feeling of fear, defiance, perhaps pity, but it will be your honest response to the other fellow in that moment. Crucially, this means an actor must agree to put their performance into the hands of another actor: your Lady Macbeth is dependent on their Macbeth; your Falstaff is dependent on their Prince Hal; your Helena is dependent on their Demetrius. This results in the maxim that *acting is reacting*.

Truthful connection to text

With Shakespeare, a reverence for the text can trap actors and directors into approaches that seek a 'right way' to give voice to his characters, searching for the right or appropriate interpretation of actions and behaviours.

Most successful theatre makers recognize and embrace the ephemerality of the art of theatre that can only create characters from the living blood and breath of actors in a particular moment. Meisner's technique is definitely incompatible with any approach that sees acting as setting aside an actor's personal experiences to seek some kind of platonic ideal of what a playwright meant a character to be, or to animate a marionette manipulated as a director determines. Meisner-trained actor and playwright David Mamet (1998: 9) captured a key Meisner principle in explaining, 'There is no character. There are only lines on a page. They are lines of dialogue meant to be said by the actor.' Every actor brings a unique treasury of personal experience to how they inhabit their lines, and for Meisner, it was crucial for an actor to draw from this treasury. He instructed his students to find 'your personal example chosen from your experience of your imagination which emotionally clarifies the cold material of the text' (1987: 138).

Meisner's focus was on developing truthful emotional connections in his actors, and he has often been seen as uninterested in text, which has led to a sense that his technique is not compatible with Shakespeare. An oft-referenced quote from Meisner, 'The text is your greatest enemy' (1987: 136), can seem hard to reconcile with a common directive from Shakespeare practitioners to 'trust the text'. Meisner, however, is not trying to discredit the work of a playwright; in fact he often emphasizes the need to trust that any playwright worth the name will give an actor the words they need when they are ready to say them. His concern instead is a caveat that an actor should not be misled by their own insecurities into trying to understand a text intellectually before they have understood it emotionally. He recognizes that the text *can* be your greatest enemy if you let your intellectual understanding dominate and close down the truthful, spontaneous responses that emerge from using the text to react truthfully to 'the other fellow'.

Meisner and Shakespeare

Meisner's interests and skills lay with modern rather than classical texts. He was sensitive to the rhythms that made modern play texts successful and saw the value of working with poetry to hone the impulses of his actors with spoken text. In working with Shakespeare, however, Meisner's techniques can only take us so far.

In opposition to Meisner's and Mamet's words, Shakespeare director and text specialist John Barton (1984: 63) said, 'The text is the character. It fills him out and gives him life.' Barton was not denying the unique emotional life an actor brings to a part, but he was always looking for balance in what an actor brings and how Shakespeare's heightened text supports the actor in finding the feelings and thoughts needed. In his survey of contemporary directing practices with Shakespeare in the US, Charles Ney (2016: 10–11) credits Barton and other text experts with 'a significant impact on the development of a generation of actors, directors and teachers ... who had realized the limits of method acting with the classics, and in particular Shakespeare'. As we will explore, if due attention is paid to how the text works, Meisner's emphasis on personal truth and response in finding the non-intellectual life of text provides a highly useful complement to how the sounds, shapes and rhythms of Shakespeare's words can support an actor's work.

Meisner may not have worked directly with Shakespeare, but one thing that comes through clearly from Longwell's first-hand account of his practice is an unquestioning assumption of Shakespeare's central role in theatre. Meisner's teaching, as reported by Longwell, is littered with examples from Shakespeare. Sometimes he uses names of characters as shortcuts to ask whether actors are responding as themselves or as a character: 'Are you talking to me now or is Lady Macbeth talking?' (1987: 19); 'Are you looking at me now . . . As Othello?' (1987: 20). At other times he illustrates a point with reference to a moment in a Shakespeare play he assumes his students will have knowledge of: 'Every play is based on the reality of doing. Even Lear's shaking his fist at the heavens – that's based on the actor thundering against fate' (1987: 25). With all his Shakespeare references, Meisner's approach is to encourage his actors to reach beyond an accepted artifice of a character and find *their* version of Lady Macbeth, of Othello, of Lear.

Formalizing Meisner's technique

Meisner himself was resistant to committing his approaches to a written format. After a first failed attempt to do so, he explains, 'I decided that a creative text book about acting was a contradiction in terms' (1987: xviii). After a second failed attempt, he explains, 'I came to realize that how I teach is determined by the gradual development of each student.' This interaction, this personal struggle of each actor which he carefully nurtured and facilitated, could not be captured through a set of exercises; hence the only direct written legacy we have of Meisner's work is a short and absorbing account of the personal struggles of one class, described by his former student Dennis Longwell. Longwell's account mainly records direct quotes from both Meisner and his students about the workings of his technique and is a must-read for anyone interested in Meisner. As intended, it gives a deep sense of the man, and the hows and whys of his technique, but not a clear account of what that technique was.

Formalizing that technique is a process others have adopted. The Sanford Meisner Centre (2020) in Los Angeles, for example, takes a particularly purist stance asserting that any deviation from Meisner's approaches, or any combining of his approaches with other acting techniques is an inferior offer designed to 'compensate for a lack of full, deep understanding of how to teach the Meisner technique properly'. Other Meisner teachers have taken on board the principles and spirit of Meisner's teaching, adapting his technique and combining it with other approaches to best serve their own community of artists, including, as this book offers, ways of working with the classic texts like Shakespeare that Meisner himself did not tend to engage with. The Neighborhood Playhouse in New York, where Meisner spent more than fifty years developing his approaches, is staffed by former pupils of the man himself and continues to offer a variety of programmes with his technique at their core, but is open to other influences and includes classes on Shakespeare.

William Esper is probably the most renowned teaching heir of Meisner's legacy. He founded the William Esper Studio in New York in 1965, continued to work closely with his mentor for nearly twenty years and has written two books, which perhaps, along with Larry Silverberg's books, come closest to recording Meisner's original teaching. Esper, however, is also keen to point out in the prologue to his first book, *The Actor's Art and Craft* (2008), that he experimented with and adapted Meisner's teachings to find his own way. In a remembered dialogue with his co-author and erstwhile student, Esper tells Damon DiMarco (2008: 4), 'If you come here, you won't be learning Meisner technique. You'll be learning my technique, the Bill Esper technique. And – God willing – if you leave here, you'll leave with your own technique.'

Scott Williams, often credited with bringing Meisner to the UK in the mid-1990s, was also taught directly by Meisner. American-born Williams trained with Meisner at the Neighborhood Playhouse in New York in the 1970s. He relocated to London in the mid-1990s, where he founded the Impulse Company and began teaching Meisner classes at the Actors Centre in 1996. Over the years of his own practice, Williams has adopted the key principles and key exercises of Meisner's work but has refined them into a five-stage process which sees Repetition as foundational. He says he teaches the 'intent of Meisner' (2020) but that his techniques are a distillation of what he finds most valuable for teaching actors today.

Mike Bernardin (2020) first learned Meisner techniques through classes with an American actor in London in 1989 but then joined forces with Williams at the Actors Centre in London around 1996. He has been acting and teaching acting ever since, keeping the essence of Meisner's work but finding his own adaptations, influenced particularly by the physical theatre of Lecoq and Decroux. Aileen Gonsalves, co-author of this book, was in turn taught by Williams and Bernardin, finding her own process from their influences and her experiences, particularly in directing Shakespeare. It is important to state that the exercises explored in this book, although firmly based in Meisner's techniques and principles, offer our interpretations and adaptations for working theatre practice today. Like Esper, we hope this will support you in developing your own practice for working with Shakespeare.

How to use this book

The approaches and exercises in this book are aimed at helping an actor find themselves in Shakespeare's text, using the principles of Meisner's technique. We encourage you to find confidence and freedom with the words and worlds of Shakespeare's plays to find the joy of responding truthfully, moment by moment within the given circumstances of Shakespeare's extraordinary texts.

We offer a short biography of Meisner in Chapter 2, describing the context of his work, with discussion about how his legacy and his approaches have been taken forward and developed by other practitioners. Chapter 3 explores Meisner's concept of 'the reality of doing' with some preliminary exercises for establishing the awareness and connection needed for a successful ensemble company working with Meisner techniques. Chapter 4 looks in more detail at Meisner's famous exercise of Repetition and how it can be used as a gateway to a more personal connection to Shakespeare's text. In Chapter 5, we review Meisner's other two key exercises of the Independent Activity and Knock on the Door, and how they support an actor in finding the reality of doing by developing the stakes that allow something to matter. Chapter 6 moves on to explore how Meisner looked at the given and imaginary circumstances of a text with exercises on creating knowledge lists from the text to develop a personal interpretation of character. Chapter 7 explores Meisner's concepts of the Preparation an actor needs so that they do not come into a scene empty, and the value of finding personal 'As Ifs' to better connect with the relationships and situations of a character.

In Chapters 8, 9 and 10, we begin to explore a reconciliation of Meisner techniques with attention to the sounds and structures of Shakespeare's heightened text. In Chapter 8, we focus on how Meisner's approaches can support the vital work of any Shakespearean actor: their approaches to line learning. Chapter 9 explores paraphrasing as an active approach to text analysis, inspired by Meisner's work, and also how Meisner's exercise of 'Breaking the Back' replaces Repetition in ways that can support an actor in speaking Shakespeare's heightened language. In Chapter 10, we discuss the strengths of working with Meisner but also the limitations of how directly helpful Meisner's techniques are when working with Shakespeare.

The final two chapters are presented in an interview format with Aileen Gonsalves, co-author of this book, in her capacity as a Meisner practitioner and Artistic Director of Butterfly Theatre Company. These chapters discuss ways forward in working with Meisner and Shakespeare developed by Butterfly Theatre Company. Chapter 11 includes an introduction to the innovative Meisner rooted process of Butterfly's Five Conditions. Chapter 12 explores how Butterfly actors find their need to speak Shakespeare's text with a confidence that allows them freedom to respond truthfully to their fellow actors in the moment. Both chapters offer additional exercises based on Butterfly's rehearsal process.

All these chapters are addressed to you, the reader, as a practitioner. Whether you are an actor, a director, a teacher, we hope you will find ideas and exercises that expand and develop your own practice. There are occasions when we address you specifically in the role of a director with that particular eye on performance, but in general we encourage you to consider, and indeed experience, the work from the different perspectives of actors, directors and teachers as you bring the texts to life.

One last note – committing this practice to cold text has not proved easy. Like any arts practice, it is far more difficult to write down in words than it is to describe and experience in a room with others. This, as all good teachers know well, is because learning is not a transmission of knowledge but an alchemical process from which we each take what we can or what we need in that moment. Just as each actor brings their own unique ideas, experiences and interpretations to the black marks on a page of a play text, so each teacher and director brings their own unique ideas, experiences and interpretations to evolving Meisner's legacy – and each person reading this book will bring their own unique ideas and experiences to adapting and evaluating the interpretation of the Meisner technique we are offering. That in fact is our best advice for how to use this book: take from it what works for you and grow that practice in your own way. No one in the whole history of humanity has the knowledge and life experiences that you have, which means no one can act like you, no one can direct like you, no one can teach like you.

We aim to help actors to:

- feel empowered to create vibrant, visceral characters through connecting to their own uniqueness;
- find permission to fully respond, moment by moment, to the text and to other actors; and
- own and share that truthful response with the audience night after night.

We aim to help directors to:

- support all actors in having their attention outwards on their fellow actors and the audience;
- work with Meisner-trained actors who particularly need to trust you to say what you see because their attention is not on self-monitoring; and
- establish a working language that can be used to change what you see in a way that helps tell the story you want to tell.

We aim to help teachers to:

- explore how using theatre-based practice creates deep analysis of Shakespeare's text in a practical, accessible way;
- support students to examine the text from the inside out as an actor does, finding their own personal connections to make the situations and relationships feel relevant to their lives; and
- enjoy a sense of journey and discovery with their students.

PART ONE

Sanford Meisner
and his work

2

Meisner's influences

Every little moment has a meaning all its own.

SANFORD MEISNER (1987: 46)

In any pursuit, arts, science, sports, we like to think of lone heroes, the genius who has access to some universal truth, the guru who can lead us to insight we could not otherwise attain. Sanford Meisner, like Stanislavsky, like Shakespeare, can sometimes be accorded this status, but it is worth remembering that each of these men were of their time. This should not take away from their achievements or the insight they have to offer, but it is always worth remembering that our identities are moulded by the culture around us and that all achievements, including those of the glove-maker's son from Stratford, are part of a social ecosystem. Of his time, Sanford Meisner was white, male and Jewish, the son of Bertha and Herman (a furrier), immigrants from Hungary. Born in 1905 in Brooklyn, and moving to South Bronx soon after, Sanford Meisner grew up in New York in the early twentieth century and was influenced by everything that meant.

Meisner himself was sensitive to how his own identity had been formed because he understood how that affected his behaviours personally and as an actor and teacher. He explains, 'I know quite clearly that the death of my brother when I was five and he was three was the dominant emotional influence in my life' (1987: 5). Finding Freud as a young man, Meisner rationalized the behaviour of his parents and his relationship with them into their blaming him and his feeling guilty for the death of his brother Jacob. Jacob's death was due to an unfortunate set of circumstances. He died from bovine tuberculosis after drinking unpasteurized milk because the family were in the countryside to improve five-year-old Sanford's health. Bertha and Herman went on to have two more children, Ruth and Robert, but it is this early experience of loss and rejection that Meisner claims as highly formative, propelling him into what he describes as an affinity with a world of fantasy (1987: 6).

Young Sanford proved to be a talented pianist and was encouraged in this pursuit, attending the Damrosch Institute of Music, now the Julliard. He received less family encouragement in his interest in acting, but this interest was fed by the fertile theatre environment of New York in the years of Meisner's adolescence. His future good friend Harold Clurman, a fellow son of non-theatre minded Jewish emigres, describes his own early theatre experiences on the lower east side of Manhattan at that time:

> The actors were among the best I have ever seen in many years of playgoing all over the world. Most stimulating of all were the audiences. For to the immigrants in the early years of the century the theatre was the one centre of social intercourse. Here the problems of their life, past and present, could be given a voice; here they could get to know and understand one another.
>
> 1975: 4

This concept of theatre as a centre of social intercourse where diverse groups can find out more about the world around them, each other, and by reflection themselves was central to the socially and politically liberal 1930s ensemble of the Group Theatre, co-led by Clurman.

The Group Theatre

When Sanford Meisner was nineteen, he talked his way into a job with the Theatre Guild as an extra in *They Knew What They Wanted*, a play written by Sidney Howard, premiering on Broadway in 1924. He subsequently took up a scholarship to study at the Theatre Guild School of Acting, despite the disapproval of his parents. At this time, Meisner met the soon to be highly influential composer Aaron Copland, another Brooklyn-born son of Jewish emigres. Unlike Meisner, however, Copland had recently studied in Paris, including classes at the Sorbonne where he had befriended

Harold Clurman. And so Clurman met Meisner, and they discovered a shared passion for theatre. Through Clurman, Meisner was drawn into a friendship group that included another passionate young actor Lee Strasberg, and a talented young producer/director Cheryl Crawford. Clurman, Crawford and Strasberg formed the now legendary Group Theatre in 1931 with twenty-eight actors invited to be founding members. Meisner was one of those actors and he credits the Group with having a profound effect on his work, as it has on the continuing practice of American theatre.

The Group Theatre proclaimed a progressive, ensemble ethos, revolutionary for its time in American theatre history. They wanted to change what theatre was about, striding into the continuing debate about theatre as entertainment or as social activism. Clurman (1975: 6) explains his sense that the theatre he saw around them 'gives itself lofty graces, claims a noble lineage' but lacked 'the best thought of our time . . . the feeling of some true personal significance'. The Group became a permanent company of individuals who spent time playing and exploring their craft together. On principle, there were to be no stars and 'capturing an idea' was a whole to be aimed for, greater than the sum of its parts of play text, actors and director (Clurman 1975: 35).

Their ensemble ideas derived from European practice mainly funnelled through Stanislavsky's emerging system. From his studies and experiences in Paris, Clurman brought influences, particularly from Stanislavsky and Coupeau. Strasberg was also deeply influenced by Stanislavsky. He, like Stella Adler, another founding member of the Group, had been deeply impressed by the performances of the Moscow Art Theatre in New York in 1923 and both had trained at the American Laboratory Theatre in the 1920s under Maria Ouspenskaya and Richard Boleslawski, who had themselves studied directly with Stanislavsky. Crawford had trained with the Theatre Guild but she also became increasingly interested in Stanislavsky's work through her association with Clurman and Strasberg, eventually meeting the man himself, and his colleague Meyerhold, on a five-week visit to Russia with Clurman in 1935. Stella Adler also spent time with Stanislavsky – in her case a concentrated five weeks of study with him in Paris that significantly clarified her understanding of his work, which she brought back to the Group.

Clurman (1975: x) describes the Group as 'reflection, image, agent, influence and product of its day'. Over the ten years of its life, between

1931 and 1941, the Group grew in influence, and produced around twenty-six contemporary plays on Broadway. Director credits for those plays are mainly Clurman and Strasberg, but also include Crawford, Meisner, Elia Kazan and Robert Lewis. Clurman (1975: 23) described the realization that motivated the Group approaches as the need to develop the actor not just as a cipher for the playwright's vision, but as personally involved in the process of creating a character: 'In our belief, unless the actor in some way shared the playwright's impulse, the result on the stage always remained somewhat mechanical.' He offers an anecdote (1975: 300) of the shift this attitude made in American theatre, describing how he met an actor in 1947, trained by Meisner, who had asked, 'Why?' when her 'old-time' director told her to make a particular move. The actor received the response: 'Don't ask me any of those arty Group Theatre questions.'

Arthur Miller describes how seeing the work of the Group inspired him and directly influenced his writing of *All My Sons*, which premiered in 1947 directed by Group alumnus Elia Kazan, and produced by Kazan and Clurman. Miller (2000: 116) writes, '*All My Sons* was begun several years after the Group has ceased to be, but it was written for what I can only call now a prophetic theatre', which he explains as expecting that a play was 'meant to become part of the lives of its audience'. Miller (2000: 115) describes how watching Group Theatre productions had given him a sense not just of brilliant ensemble acting, but also of an 'air of union created between actors and audience . . . it was possible to feel the heat and the passion of people moved not only in their bellies but in their thoughts'. In 1938, the Group took a production of Clifford Odets' *Golden Boy* (featuring Meisner as the gangster Eddie Fuseli) to London. A review in *The Times* captured a response from London audiences, who recognized a different energy and connection about the ensemble acting: 'The acting attains a level which is something we know nothing at all about' (cited in Clurman 1975: 225). Meisner continued as an active member of the Group until it broke up in 1941.

The Group Theatre's legacy

In his Epilogue to *The Fervent Years*, his account of the life of the Group, Clurman (1975: 320) gives his definition of theatre, as he believed the Group achieved it:

For the theatre is not a business; it never has been basically that. It is an art of direct communication grounded on shared social and moral values. It is not, first of all, a condiment, a genteel pastime, an escape from reality, but like all art it is a resource in civilization's human treasury.

Meisner (1987: 11) describes the exercises that make up his technique as 'designed to strengthen the guiding principle that I learned forcefully in the Group – that art expresses human experience – which principle I have never, and will never, give up'.

The legacy of the Group is huge and each member took the Stanislavsky techniques they had explored into their own evolution of what acting means. In his epilogue to *The Fervent Years*, Clurman (1975: 300) heralds a key legacy of the Group's work: 'The Stanislavsky "method", once considered a foreign excrescence in the American theatre has developed, in one form or another, into the prevalent method for training the young actor in drama schools, "studios" and colleges.' Cheryl Crawford, Elia Kazan and Robert Lewis went on to found the Actors Studio in 1947, joined by Lee Strasberg in 1951. Stella Adler set up her own Studio of Acting in 1949 and her technique continues to be highly influential. Meisner joined the Neighborhood Playhouse in 1935. His role there came about because Clifford Odets, another Group member, became too busy to direct a final year student production at the Playhouse and suggested Meisner take the job instead of him. At the Playhouse, Meisner found his vocation as a teacher and the space to be able to develop his own techniques.

Like other members of the Group, Meisner spent time in Los Angeles under the lure of Hollywood. He moved there in 1959 to become a film actor and director of the New Talent Division for Twentieth Century Fox. But by 1962, he was back in New York, back to the classroom and the theatre world where he felt most fulfilled. Although he was an acclaimed actor and director, he himself claimed to feel most at home in the classroom. He briefly taught acting at the American Musical Theatre Academy, before returning to the Neighborhood Playhouse in 1964. He remained there until his retirement in 1990, and even then stayed active as Director Emeritus of the Acting Department until his death in 1997. The Neighborhood Playhouse, where Meisner spent more than fifty years developing his approaches, now heralds itself as 'The home of the Meisner technique'.

Meisner and Stanislavsky

The core of the various approaches of Method Acting developed by Group alumni can perhaps be found in Meisner's (1987: 169) 'in a nutshell' description: 'the process of filling a cold text with your life', the key word here being 'your'. Where actor development had previously focused on the necessary physical skills of voice and movement, the seismic shift following the influence of Stanislavsky's System was to develop the mental skills of the actor and their ability to bring their own emotional life to their playing of a role. Meisner's process is deeply influenced by Stanislavsky; unlike other members of the Group, however, Meisner had no direct contact with the man himself. He learned of the Russian practice initially from Clurman, Strasberg and Adler, and later from acclaimed actor/director Michael Chekov, who moved to the US in the 1940s. Additionally, as Phillipa Strandberg-Long (2018) outlines, Meisner had access to the writing of Stanislavsky's contemporaries, director/theorists Sudakov and Rapoport. Their influence can be seen particularly in Rapoport's focus on 'outward attention', which he used to build living relationships in the moment, and Sudakov's concept of 'the reality of doing', a phrase Meisner often used. Stanislavsky's influence on world theatre now looms so large that it is hard to find any Western acting technique that does not build from it in some way. His work has often, however, been summarized and formalized, perhaps giving the impression of more rigidity of thought than actually existed. Former Meisner student David Mamet (1998: 15) even regards him as a 'dilettante' with ideas now unworkable. Meisner himself seems deeply respectful of Stanislavsky's work, as will be noted further in later chapters, but he interpreted and developed that inheritance in his own way for his own time.

Following Stanislavsky, other Group Theatre-inspired practices begin with connection to the character and how a composite of actor and character might behave. Meisner's particular development was to see an actor's performance as dependent on his fellow actors. While all actors and directors are looking for connection, it is on this crucial point of *starting* with that focus on emotional connection between actors that Meisner differs from his erstwhile Group Theatre colleagues. Scott Williams describes his teaching of Meisner as about being 'a kind of muscular development' for actors 'in observing and responding in a 50-50 balance', so that observing others feeds your own behaviour as much as any Stanislavsky or Method-inspired internal knowledge. He describes the key difference of Meisner as about where you are looking: 'are you looking inside or out at the other person?'

Stella Adler explains how 'Mr Stanislavsky had *his* Method. Do you understand?' She means Stanislavsky, like any good director and teacher, was a reflective practitioner, always exploring new ways to bring out the best in his actors and students. One of his most oft quoted (though unattributed) lines exemplifies this: 'Create your own method. Don't depend slavishly on mine. Make up something that will work for you! But keep breaking traditions, I beg you.' Meisner had great respect for Adler, and great respect, like her, for the art of teaching as well as of acting. Meisner saw the strength of what he had to offer in the art of personal relationships, not in devising a set formula that any actor can follow.

Meisner and Method

The concept of Method Acting came out of the explorations of the Group Theatre in the 1930s but has become most well-known through alumni of the Actors Studio, and in particular Lee Strasberg. Meisner first worked as a young actor with Strasberg in the Theatre Guild and then in the Group Theatre, until Strasberg left in 1937. Strasberg later rejoined his former colleagues, Crawford and Clurman, at the Actors Studio, taking up its directorship in 1951. Since then his name has become synonymous with a particular formula for Method Acting. Meisner (1987: 82–4) was dismissive of Strasberg's achievements, believing his skill lay more in talent spotting and claiming credit for that talent rather than in developing it, a judgement Mamet (1998: 14) also takes: 'the Actors' Studio, in the fifties arrogated to itself some fine talents. The Studio, however, chose them, it did not make them.'

The Lee Strasberg Theatre and Film Institute (LSTFI) has homes in both New York and Los Angeles, and, with something of a religious fervour, describes itself as 'the only school that teaches Lee Strasberg's work in its complete and authentic form'. The LSTFI proclaims its aim as 'to provide students with a craft that will help them create a reality and respond truthfully in imaginary circumstances'. This sounds remarkably like the aim of a Meisner programme, but the two men developed very different processes. One of Meisner's students, Ray, studied under both. He comments that Meisner's process of getting an actor's attention out and on to 'the other fellow' seems the opposite of what he had been told by Strasberg, whose approach was, he says, to 'make you go inside', adding, 'and you can get stuck in there'. Meisner agrees: 'I told Lee that when he was alive. I said to him. "You introvert the already introverted"' (1987: 59).

The core element that Strasberg kept hold of from his studies of the Stanislavsky System at the American Laboratory Theatre was 'affective' or 'emotion memory' – that actors should summon their own deepest emotional memories and exploit those feelings to give life to their characters. It was Strasberg's continued attachment to 'emotion memory' that led to artistic differences with his erstwhile comrades in Stanislavskian arms, particularly Stella Adler. Adler spent five weeks with Stanislavsky in Paris in 1934 and learned that he had evolved his ideas, putting greater emphasis on an actor's *imagination* to create emotion and live under the given circumstances of a text, rather than reanimating possibly troubling and difficult personal memories, memories which in any case change over time. She brought her findings back to the Group. Meisner (1987: 79) describes that lesson in his own way:

In the early days of the Stanislavsky system, Mr S was looking for true behaviour, and if what he wanted was great pleasure, he asked where you look for the reality of great pleasure. His answer was simple: you *remember* great pleasure. That's called 'emotion memory'. I don't use it and neither did he after thirty years of experimentation. The reason? If you are twenty and work in a delicatessen, the chances are very slim that you can remember the glorious night you had with Sophia Loren ... what you're looking for is not necessarily confined to the reality of your life. It can be in your imagination. If you allow it freedom – with no inhibitions, no properties – to imagine what would happen between you and Sophia Loren, your imagination is, in all likelihood, deeper and more persuasive than the real experience.

Strasberg was not convinced and, perhaps not coincidentally, left the Group soon after Adler's return.

Another key tenet of Strasberg's teaching of the Method puts heavy emphasis on backstory. Meisner (1987: 74–5) pokes fun at how the intensity of such an approach can result in an actor spending six months 'seeing the snow' before they can authentically deliver the line, 'Look at the snow', as they look out of an onstage window at what in reality is probably scenery stacked up against a wall. Meisner encourages his actors to create backstories in the process of interrogating a text (see 'Connecting to the given circumstances', page 53), but his emphasis is on the authentic emotional delivery of a line, resulting from what the actor imagines it *means* for the character to see the snow in that moment, rather than constructing a whole life for the character leading up to that moment. Meisner believes an audience make sense of a moment of performance through how the actor responds. He explains, 'So as a convention, you walk to the window to make the audience believe that you're looking out. It's for the *audience*, not for you! And what it means to you is something emotional: *'I'll lose my job!'* You follow?' (1987: 75, italics original). Because of the context of the play, the audience associate the actions of walking to the window, looking out and saying the line, 'Look at the snow', with the actor's feelings engendered by imagining losing their job. The character's circumstances may be a sense of loss over something other than a job, but imagining losing the job might be what works best for the actor to find the right response. This association of the actor's feelings with the playwright's words and associated actions results in what Mamet (1997: 9, 21) calls 'the illusion of character'.

Meisner's work was closer to Stella Adler's and her description of acting as 'an effort that goes out toward the audience, not something merely self-reverential' (2000: 265). Adler's work builds on Stanislavsky's later developments on 'The Method of Physical Acting' and the 'Active Analysis' he was working towards when she met him near the end of his life. Meisner (1987: 183) admired her greatly and built on her interpretations. He notes, however, 'though Stella doesn't teach the way I do'. Rose Marie, a student who studied under both Adler and Meisner, agrees: 'Not at all!' Meisner's techniques found something like Stanislavsky's concept of *communion* – how actors develop energy channels of communication if they open themselves up to each other's personal impulses, discovered through the physical actions of their character's journey through a play. Strandberg-Long (2018: 14) argues that 'communion was in fact the starting point of both Meisner's technique and Stanislavsky's latter work'.

Meisner's passion, what he described (1987: 160) as his 'biggest job in teaching', was in bringing actors together with themselves so that they could interpret material from their hearts rather than their heads and open up such channels of communication with each other. While recognizing that everyone is different, Meisner developed a set of foundational exercises to support this process. These exercises, along with an exploration of the principles and advice he offered to accompany them, are explored in subsequent chapters.

Meisner's timeline

1905 – Born in Brooklyn to Bertha and Herman Meisner, Jewish immigrants from Hungary.

1910 – His brother Jacob died in an accident for which Meisner was made to feel responsible.

1924 – Performed as an extra in *They Knew What They Wanted* and subsequently took up a scholarship to study at the Theatre Guild School of Acting.

1926 – Met Harold Clurman.

1931 – Became one of twenty-eight actors who were founding members of the Group Theatre, established by Harold Clurman, Cheryl Crawford and Lee Strasberg.

1931–41 – The Group Theatre grew in influence, and produced around twenty-six contemporary plays on Broadway.

1935 – Began teaching at the Neighborhood Playhouse in New York.

1941 – Left the Group Theatre as it disbanded.

1959 – Moved to Los Angeles to become a film actor and director of the New Talent Division for Twentieth Century Fox.

1962 – Moved back to New York and taught at the American Musical Theatre Academy.

1964 – Returned to teach at the Neighborhood Playhouse.

1990 – Retired.

1997 – Died.

3

The reality of doing

The foundation of acting is the reality of doing.

SANFORD MEISNER (1987: 16)

Meisner regarded 'the reality of doing' as 'the basis, the foundation of acting' (1987: 25). His first exercise with a new class is to ask them to listen for a minute for how many cars they can hear outside the building. His key question in interrogating his students' answers is: 'Did you listen for yourself or were you playing some character?' (1987: 17). Next he asks them to sing a tune to themselves in their own heads and then to count the number of light bulbs in the room. With each of these simple tasks, he wants his students to try the task unself-consciously without any regard for being watched in the process or for how their responses might be judged. He wants them to focus on really doing the task, not indicating they are doing it by bobbing their heads, tapping their fingers or other conscious behaviours, making the point that if you are really doing something you are focused on that activity, not on superficially trying to make it interesting for an audience or doing what you think your character would do. As one of his students explains, 'If you're really doing it, then you don't have time to watch yourself doing it. You only have the time and energy to do it' (Meisner 1987: 24).

Meisner's key example (1987: 14–15) in illustrating the 'reality of doing' is George Bernard Shaw's 1895 review of Eleonora Duse's performance of Magda in *Heimat* by Hermann Sudermann. In the review, Shaw is deeply impressed by the extent to which Duse is physically affected by her own dramatic imagination. In the play, Magda is put in the very difficult situation of unexpectedly meeting the estranged father of her child in her own father's house. Duse's reactions include a blush which she attempts to hide from her former lover. Meisner describes this in his own words: 'All of a sudden she realizes that she's blushing, and it gets so bad that she drops her head and hides her face in embarrassment. Now that's a piece of realistic acting!' Meisner is effusive in his praise of Duse's blush because he regards it as 'the epitome of living truthfully under imaginary circumstances'. Since a blush is not easily induced, Duse is not 'acting' her anxiety at meeting her former lover but living in the moment, fully engaged in her 'reality of doing' as Magda.

Silent messages – the '93 per cent rule'

In a book called *Silent Messages: Implicit Communication of Emotions and Attitudes*, first published in 1981, Albert Mehrabian explored the importance of non-verbal aspects of communication including tone of voice, facial expressions and body language. From research he carried out about how people express whether they like or dislike things, he concluded that only 7 per cent of their emotional attitude is communicated through the words they used, 38 per cent through their tone of voice and 55 per cent through their facial expressions and other physical gestures. Although these statistics applied only to a very particular set of experiments, they have been taken up by many to claim that human communication is 93 per cent about how we express language, and only 7 per cent about the actual words we use. Subsequent studies have shown that we do gain a significant amount of our understanding through non-verbal or paralinguistic aspects of communication, and although what has become known as the 7-38-55 rule of communication should not be regarded as a statistical fact, it can be a useful shorthand reminder of just how much human communication is non-verbal.

Stanislavsky (1981: 101) recognized that 'The speech of the eyes and face is so subtle that it conveys emotions, thoughts, feelings, with scarcely perceptible muscular movements.' We do not know whether Meisner was aware of Mehrabian's theory but we do know that he built on Stanislavsky's work, developing techniques that are based firmly in the observable truth of such barely perceptible 'silent messages'. Meisner's exercise of Repetition is designed to diminish the importance of the words spoken, focusing instead on *how* those words are spoken and the emotional responses that *how* brings out.

The basic ideas of Mehrabian's '93 per cent rule' can be a useful shorthand for this focus and for understanding Meisner's concept of the reality of doing. The 'silent message' of Duse's blush was far more affecting for Shaw than any of the words she spoke.

Particularly interesting for actors is that Mehrabian's original research looks at what happens when verbal and non-verbal communication contradict each other. If someone says they like your hair but their tone and/or movements suggest otherwise, would you believe them? Subsequent research supports Mehrabian's early findings that we believe visual evidence first – how somebody appears and behaves; then vocal – their tone and use of voice; and finally verbal – what they actually say. Meisner's techniques support an actor in understanding and manipulating this balance of priorities in human communication by focusing on the non-verbal '93 per cent'.

The remaining verbal '7 per cent' was not Meisner's priority but, as will be discussed further in this book, that is a limitation of his work for the Shakespearean actor. For an actor to do full justice to Shakespeare, they need to recognize the detail of what the text gives them – what Cicely Berry (2008: 16) describes as 'the specificity of the word itself, for no other word will do'. Human civilization is built on this specificity of words that allows us to communicate in far greater detail than any other animal. To appreciate the value of words in the '93 per cent rule', we might consider that we share around 96 per cent of our DNA with chimpanzees. That 4 per cent makes a big difference, it makes us human and it includes our capacity for verbal language.

Act before you think

John: We're so conditioned to keep everything in. Now, all of a sudden, it's our job to let everything out.
Meisner: That, my friends, is why we're all here.
MEISNER AND LONGWELL 1987: 116

Meisner illustrates his key principles of *'Don't do anything unless something happens to make you do it'* and *'What you do doesn't depend on you; it depends on the other fellow'*, quite literally (1987: 34–5, italics original). Giving a student a line to speak: 'Mr Meisner', he asks the student to turn away from him. He then reaches out and pinches the student on the back. The student jumps away, yelling his line in surprise. This, explains Meisner, is a truthful response: 'my pinch justified their ouch ... And their ouch was the direct result of my pinch.' This physical example then becomes a metaphor running through his work as he encourages his actors to develop the acting muscles of *pinch and ouch*.

Meisner was adamant that the reality of doing means that an actor needs to work from instincts, from our truthful emotional responses to any situation before we regulate our behaviour according to social norms. He advises his actors: 'never pick material in response to your ambition or your intellect. You should pick material that comes out of your gut.' He then adds, 'Unless you need a job' (1987: 163). He knew that, despite the best ambitions of theatre practitioners, the world of theatre is not an ideal. Because, however, the best acting comes from your gut, if you take on a role that does not immediately resonate with you, you have to work harder to find those personal connections. Finding those connections means developing a professional disregard for the regulations of socially accepted behaviour that we are all subject to in real life. Creating an atmosphere in a rehearsal room that inspires you to take the risk to 'fuck polite', as Meisner (1987: 33) graphically put it, is very important when rehearsing any production, but particularly when rehearsing Shakespeare. It allows everyone to be less self-conscious, less worried that you are 'getting it right', and reminds you that you are creating a unique Shakespeare production that needs each individual to be themselves and to be connected to each other, not just to the text.

After illustrating his concept of 'the reality of doing' through simple listening and counting exercises, Meisner introduces a listing exercise, asking one student to list everything they observe about another student sitting next to them. He then builds these observations into his key exercise of Repetition (explored in the next chapter). The following three exercises build on the principles of 'the reality of doing' and explore the '93 per cent rule' as preliminary exercises to help you train your attention outwards so that you are really doing a task rather than watching yourself do the task. These exercises develop your ability to see clearly, and respond honestly from your point of view. They are useful exercises to do in the early stages of rehearsal for a Shakespeare play or when studying scenes, as they help you bond as an ensemble, create a working language, and build permission and trust.

Exercise 1: The reality of doing

1 Choose something that has multiple things to it and would need your full attention to count it properly. For example: the railings of a radiator, the slats on blinds, the squares in a pattern on the floor, the stacked chairs in the corner.

2 After everyone in the group has counted individually, have only one person count while everyone else watches them.

3 Discuss whether the person counting noticed anything different about how they counted. Is it different when you know you are being watched? What did the observers see – someone really counting or 'acting' counting? How does this affect your experience as an observer?

You can repeat the exercise by trying to count the number of cars that you can hear going past or other sounds. This helps to train your attention fully outward and to make you specific in *really doing* whatever you are doing.

Exercise 2: Building permission

1 Walk around the room. You cannot talk. Remember no one can read your mind!

2 Check out other people's shoes, run your eyes over their whole body from their shoes up to their hair and finally, when you clock each other's eyes, take permission to do whatever the person you are looking at makes you want to do. It might be to play with their hair or pull a toggle, hug or smile or examine a necklace. At first you may be cautious but as it goes on you will gain more permission. And remember, no one should passively accept other people's actions – you can engage or you can pull away.

3 Discuss what it was like to do. It's fine to either love or hate it. You will have gained an understanding of the difference between being in and out of your head – self-conscious or

present and responsive. You will also have discovered how much or how little permission you feel with each other. Discuss what seemed to be habitual, polite behaviour and what seemed impulsive, authentic behaviour.

This exercise allows you to discover your unique point of view. No one out of all the billions on this planet, indeed no one in the whole of human history, nor the future of humanity, is the same as you. You are unique, and it is that uniqueness that will make your responses and therefore your characters, unique.

Exercise 3: Listing

This exercise helps you realize how much more there is to see in the other person than you first perceive. It's helpful for a director to lead and note various discoveries.

1 Two actors stand opposite each other. Name one person A and one B. Everyone else observes B and tries to see what A has missed.

2 A closes their eyes and then opens them and names every piece of behaviour out loud that they see B do for thirty seconds. Then they swap over. These calls might be: You blinked, You frowned, You smiled, You moved your head, etc.

3 The observers discuss what A has missed.

The director counts only the blinks and alerts everyone to the fact they missed, for example, thirteen blinks. Discuss why people don't say *all* the blinks. Answers may include: because it's everyday, it's natural, it's boring, etc. We censor ourselves all the time and after a while we don't bother naming everything, but the danger is we stop noticing everything. This exercise helps us see clearly. Do it again with the lister naming absolutely everything – they will not be able to stop talking as so much happens. Even supposed total stillness is a call to make. In this exercise you become too busy to be self-conscious and you realize your acting partner is always doing something. As a responsive actor, your job is to consider whether that is something good or bad for your objective. The more you can see as an actor, the more you have to respond to.

Summary of reality of doing

- Meisner regarded 'the reality of doing' as 'the basis, the foundation of acting' (1987: 25).

- This means really doing a task without being self-conscious and without exaggerating your behaviour to show you are doing a task.

- Meisner helps you see how much communication lays beneath the words someone speaks (the '93 per cent') and how much of our day-to-day behaviour is regulated by social norms. An actor needs to professionally disregard socially polite behaviour in order to inhabit the point of view of their character.

- The reality of doing leads to Meisner's metaphor of 'pinch and ouch' – that an actor responding truthfully is like being pinched and yelling ouch.

- This work can make you more aware of how learned habitual responses can stop us seeing clearly and responding truthfully.

4

Repetition

*My pinch justified their ouch ... And their ouch was the
direct result of my pinch,*

SANFORD MEISNER (1987: 35)

Repetition is an exercise fundamental to Meisner's technique. He
developed it in his classes in the late 1950s and early 1960s, and
regarded it as the opposite of the introspection of Strasberg's
Method because its purpose is to establish connection with another
actor, through actively listening and repeating what they say.
Meisner teachers have evolved the activity in their own ways and
different opinions have arisen over whether it is right to name
emotions ('You're excited') and judge behaviours ('You look bored')
or just to observe what seems factually true ('You're smiling' / 'You
sighed'). We discuss these differences below in the section on
observation versus judgement. First is a summary of Meisner's own
approach, adapted from Longwell's account, recording three stages
of what he calls 'The Word Repetition Game'. Meisner practitioners
generally just call it Repetition and throughout this book we use
Repetition as a proper noun to distinguish the Meisner exercise
from the normal use of the word.

Meisner's word repetition game

Stage 1: Two actors face each other. One begins by saying something
aloud that they observe as being true of the other. For example:
'Your hair is shiny' or 'You're blinking.' The second repeats this line

exactly as they hear it: 'Your hair is shiny.' The first repeats the line again exactly as they heard it from the second and so they go on until told to stop. Meisner (1987: 22) demands that they do not introduce any variety. He explains, 'It's mechanical and inhuman, but it's the basis for something' – that something being 'what eventually becomes emotional dialogue.'

Stage 2: In the next stage, Meisner asks for the two actors to repeat the lines from their own point of view, changing the pronoun. For example: 'You're staring at me' / 'I'm staring at you' / 'You're staring at me . . .' Meisner (1987: 23) points out how this simple shift has made the mechanical and inhuman Repetition into something more like human conversation.

Stage 3: Actors are allowed to change the call and say something else that they observe about their partner. For example: 'You're staring at me' / 'I'm staring at you' / 'You're staring at me' / 'I'm staring at you' / 'You admit it?' / 'I admit it' / 'You admit it?' / 'I admit it' / 'I don't like it' / 'You don't like it.' These call changes should come instinctively as a response to your partner's shifting behaviour. You should never have to think about what to say next, either you repeat what your partner has said or you change the call without thinking.

Once this exercise has been established, you can play around with it. For example, Meisner asks two actors to face away from each other. He then asks one actor to do something that makes the other actor respond. The actors then go into Repetition, for example: 'You poked me in the back' / 'I poked you in the back' / 'You poked me in the back' / 'Yes, I poked you in the back' / 'What's funny?' / 'What's funny?' Meisner (1987: 26–30) insists that any change in the Repetition comes from an instinct, an emotional response, and not merely a desire to add variety.

Why do Repetition?

Meisner (1987: 36) describes how he developed the exercise as a reaction to the improvisations of the early days of the Group Theatre. He tells Longwell, 'These were general verbalizations of what we thought was an approximation of our situation in the play. We were retelling what we remembered of the story of the play using our own words. I came to the realization that this was all intellectual nonsense.' While these improvisations were following Stanislavsky's ideas of establishing the given circumstances of the text before moving into the inner life of the characters, Meisner wanted to reach immediately into an actor's heart. He continues: 'I decided I wanted an exercise for actors where there is no intellectuality. I wanted to eliminate all that "head" work, to take away all the mental manipulation and get to where the impulses come from.'

Meisner (1987: 36–7) describes the value of Repetition as eliminating the need to think 'and to write dialogue out of your head in order to keep talking'. Quite simply it gives you something to say and then to discover that *how* you say it is, at this stage, more important than *what* you say. The repetitive back and forth of lines in Repetition is not about performance but instead about training an actor to become more aware of their subconscious responses to the behaviour of others. Neuro-scientific research has revealed how our brains pick up on myriad small cues in a fellow human that allow us to assess that person's emotional state. This is thought to activate 'mirror neurons' in our brains that simulate how we would feel if we exhibited those same responses, which helps us to understand how they might be feeling. It is probable that mirror neurons evolved as 'an unconscious system for monitoring the intentions of others' (Trimble, 2012: 108), a highly useful skill for such a socially dependent species as humans. Intention being the stuff of acting, this is interesting to note. We can never actually know how someone else is feeling and should remember that any assessments we make come from our own perspective with all the cultural biases and past experiences we bring to that moment. That is why we can only respond to each other from *our own point of view*. It is, however, very useful for us to assess how someone else *might* be feeling because of how they might then behave and how that might affect us.

It is this fundamental human skill that Meisner's Repetition exercise develops. As the Repetition bounces backwards and forwards between the actors, they are learning how to notice all the tiny physiological cues their partner is giving out. It is important that they notice everything about their partner: the tiniest bead of sweat, the smallest curling of a finger, how fast they blink. This close observation activates an actor's mirror neurons to assess how the other person is feeling and this triggers their own impulses in how to respond. Scott Williams describes this as a 'seemingly endless exercise [that] develops a set of musculature in the actor which says I'm here to observe you almost clinically and respond impulsively to that which I see'. Through the exercise, actors learn to funnel their emotional responses, fine-tuning them into intuitions that allow them to respond truthfully moment to moment from the heart rather than the head. Meisner (1987: 107) tells his students, 'The illogical nature of the dialogue opened you up to the impulsive shifts in your instinctual behaviour caused by what was being done to you by your partner which can lead to real emotion. This is fundamental to good acting.'

Observations versus judgements

Scott Williams' emphasis is to focus on calls that are observations rather than judgements. Statements like 'You're blinking', 'You're smiling' or 'You're shrugging' are tangible, precise and unarguable. Other Meisner practitioners encourage calls that observe an emotion rather than simply an action: 'You're angry', 'You look happy', 'You make me feel sad', 'You're making me annoyed.' Williams believes that a call from a point of view in this way can only ever be 'speculation' and tends to guide the work into 'what I think I feel from what you are giving me', which pushes too much towards ways in which the intellect leads.

The advantage of following Williams' rule of observable physical actions only is that it avoids straying into the nuanced territory of labelling behaviours with emotions. If while doing Repetition, the actor makes an emotional call, and the director asks, 'Why did you say they were angry?', the answer will be because they frowned or shouted, or screwed up their face. Any such response can be verified by others watching as a truthful observation. Whether or not someone is angry is difficult to establish as a simple truth, often even for the person being described in such a way. Scientific study of behaviour often distinguishes between 'emotions' as universal categories and 'feelings' as personal, individual experiences, usually a cocktail of different emotions. Naming an emotion can put an actor in their head as they seek to find the right word, and can put the labelled actor in their head as they have to think, 'Am I angry?' An exercise that is not about the words, but about finding instinctive impulses, can then become all about the words. It can also create disputes which are unhelpful, whereas simply using objectively verifiable, tangible observations, as Williams says, 'makes for a happier world'.

It is worth noting that Meisner, himself, is untroubled by this. When a student asks him, 'If he looks bored I could say, "You look bored"? I could make a judgement?', Meisner responds, 'Of his behaviour, yes' (1987: 29). Meisner's primary objective with the exercise is to open up his actors' instinctive impulses in order to respond truthfully rather than suppressing those impulses to what is socially acceptable or appropriate. In everyday life we are often too circumspect to say 'You're angry at me' when we hear annoyance in someone's voice. Meisner asks his actors to call what they see from their own perspective. Their partner then has the opportunity to restate or confirm this judgement: 'You think I'm angry with you', or 'I'm angry at you' or whatever makes most sense for them in that moment. Mike Bernardin, an experienced Meisner teacher, prefers to offer his students the freedom to make calls that label an emotion when he feels his actors can fully recognize their partner's behaviour. He suggests that if you can see clearly that from your point of view the person opposite you is angry, not calling that is what can feel untruthful. He explains, 'Sometimes you have to say it out loud in order to grapple with it.' If that call seems unarguable to you, you can make it, partly because it helps you to discover in the moment what your own response to that behaviour is.

Through experimentation you will find what works best for you and whether calls that name emotions are useful or distracting. As working practice, it is more important to use the spirit of Meisner's principles of being flexible and responsive in the moment to connect, rather than attempting to find the purity of a Meisner technique. Meisner emphasized that his practice was dependent on who was in front of him at the time. Bernardin, for example, asks his students to make their Repetition 'fast and loud' or to hold hands, whatever is needed for them to find their connection.

Why do Repetition when working with Shakespeare?

Repetition is commonly used to open up actors' emotions and develop their instinctive responses to each other. Williams describes

Repetition as about 'repeating syllables that effectively become nonsense though they begin in observation'. Their use is simply to give the actor something to say that becomes part of whatever emotional behaviour is happening between the two actors. Repetition can also, however, build a foundational relationship to text work. The more meaningless the words at the Repetition stage, the more likely that actors will express themselves by speaking with how they feel, which by default expands their tone and range of voice, as well as their physical responses. Once you feel empowered to see clearly and respond honestly from your own point of view as you speak the words in Repetition, it becomes a natural step towards seeing clearly and responding honestly from your character's point of view as you speak the words provided by the text. You are then free to respond to the emotion of the situation rather than your intellectual understanding of the text.

Bernardin (2020) takes his actors through stages of working with Repetition where the language gradually becomes more important. As his students become more confident, he allows calls that become self-referential, labelling their own emotion in order to provoke a behavioural shift in their partner. He explains:

> I'm trying to get to a point where the Repetition is so fluid and the attention is so habitually fixed on the other person that I can say, 'You're really scaring me' and not have my attention come back to roost with me, but what I'm doing by saying that is I'm confronting the other person with a truth they don't seem to be dealing with.

In this way, Bernardin creates a stepping stone towards working with text by building recognition in his actors that 'The language itself is an agent of change and communication.' While maintaining the fundamental Meisner approach that Repetition teaches you to focus your attention out onto your partner and to speak with how you feel, Bernardin's process brings back in the fact that words also matter.

The value of Repetition is in recognizing that human beings are predisposed to read each other's responses and attach emotions to those responses based on their own feelings. The need and desire to share this emotional understanding is regarded by many as key to the development of words from sounds, resulting in our very human, integrated continuum of verbal and non-verbal language. Meisner's passion was in fine-tuning those instincts to create emotionally vibrant actors who are highly responsive, moment to moment, depending on each other for their performances.

Exercises with Repetition

Try the following exercises using Repetition with calls from your own point of view, (as described above in 'Stage 2' under the subheading 'Meisner's Word Repetition Game'). These exercises help actors understand how to connect truthfully under the various given circumstances that the text, director's vision, staging, accents and costume can demand.

Exercise 1: Repetition with constraints

- Stand opposite your partner as far across the room as you can.
- One actor begins by saying something aloud that they observe as being true of the other. The second repeats this line from their own point of view. Each actor can change the call according to the other person's shifting behaviour. For example: 'You're blinking' / 'I'm blinking'; 'You're blinking' / 'I'm blinking'; 'You smiled' / 'I smiled'; 'You smiled' / 'I smiled' . . .
- Speak with your voice raised to reach your partner. Don't allow the volume to drop.
- After a few minutes, stop and start again following the instructions above but this time whispering to each other without raising your voice at any time.
- Again, after a few minutes, stop and start the Repetition again but this time stand side by side with your partner. You are allowed to touch but you cannot make eye contact with them.
- Start again with Repetition, sitting at a table opposite your partner. You have to keep your hands on the table and you are not allowed to move your hands or stand up.

After each of these variations, discuss what difference the constraint made from the perspective of the actors and from the perspective of any observers. Staging constraints like these are inherent in many Shakespeare scenes. For example in *Macbeth* 3.4, the 'banquet' scene, Macbeth and Lady Macbeth try to have a private conversation surrounded by the assembled court about the sudden appearance of Banquo's ghost. In *Twelfth Night* 2.5, the 'letter' scene, Sir Toby, Sir Andrew and Fabian have to whisper while hiding and spying on Malvolio. Repetition with fixed constraints allows you to explore what is happening underneath the text when affected by the constraint.

Exercise 2: Three-hander Repetition

- Three actors stand in a triangle facing each other. One begins Repetition (as outlined in Exercise 1 above), addressed to one other actor. That second actor responds and the Repetition continues as normal.

- At some point the third actor will feel an impulse to interject with a response addressed to one of the other two. The actor addressed then responds and the Repetition continues, bouncing between all three actors.

- All actors should feel permission to speak with how they feel at all times and do what the others make them want to do. That might mean jumping between the others to interrupt because often the truthful feeling is one of being left out – or walking away.

This exercise gets you into the habit of responding truthfully with conflicting responses to more than one person at a time. In *Two Gentlemen of Verona* 2.4, for example, Silvia and her secret beloved are saddled with Thurio who is her unwanted persistent suitor, and the shifts in dialogue between them are interesting to explore. When Thurio leaves, Proteus, Valentine's best friend, arrives. He falls for Silvia at first sight and another three-hander scene continues with a different dynamic to explore. The moment-to-moment shifts and tears can be explored as Proteus tries to hide his true feelings of desire for her and jealousy of his best friend. Before working on the text, it is both fun and useful to try Repetition to explore the pulls

REPETITION   39

and tears that come up. It is always helpful to have observers who can comment on what they notice about how alliances will shift as tone and behaviour are affected as the Repetition dances between the three actors.

Exercise 3: Repetition adding accents

- Try Repetition with a partner (as outlined in Exercise 1 above) using your own accent.
- Then try with the same partner with both of you adding an accent.

Plays often require actors to use accents, but this can make actors feel self-conscious. Doing Repetition with the accent in place can help keep your attention outwards. Observers may notice how different accents somehow change the words the actors unconsciously choose to use. For example when doing an upper-class accent, observers might comment on how the actor instinctively adds words such as 'really' or 'yes' and say, 'Yes, I am indeed blinking', rather than just 'I'm blinking'. It's as if there's an inherent entitlement that the accent allows and seems to happen unconsciously. In the same way with a lower-class accent, actors might unconsciously add different words such as: 'Ok I'm blinking' or 'Yeah I'm blinking' and can be less precise in repeating the exact words. It is very liberating for actors to do Repetition using their characters' accents before using their actual text. This allows them to be less self-conscious in exploring how the accent transforms them physically and affects how much permission they feel they have in how they speak to their partner. This exploration of how accents affect status can be very useful in working with Shakespeare, for example in *As You Like It* with scenes between the characters of the court and those who live in the forest.

Exercise 4: Repetition adding costumes

- Try Repetition with a partner (as outlined in Exercise 1 above) wearing your own normal clothes.
- Get into costume or simply add a signifier such as a cloak or a crown.

- Walk around the room on your own and let the costume
  affect you. The weight of a crown may unbalance you or
  force you to be more stiff and upright to keep it in place.
  The heaviness of a cloak might ground you in a different
  way; it might make you feel more dominant or you might
  enjoy flourishing it as you command the space.
- Then try Repetition with the same partner and note any
  differences in how you respond.

Costumes can have a huge impact on how you see clearly and
respond honestly, as they will affect your point of view. Observers
may notice how certain clothes give or take away permission in this
exercise for the wearer but also for those they interact with in the
exercise. For example, wearing a crown may make others defer to
you or add flourishes to your physical movements. The tightness of
a corset or layers of petticoats often found in traditional Shakespeare
dress affect how much permission or constraint you feel. It is
entirely unique for each actor. It may also affect your word choice
in Repetition as with accents.

Women in disguise dressing as men can be found in many
Shakespeare plays. It is useful for actors playing these parts to
experiment with Repetition with their 'male' costume, as it can
really help them find their physicality and tone of voice by allowing
the costume to affect them while interacting and responding to each
other.

Exercise 5: Repetition with staging restrictions

- Two actors are separated from each other by a physical
  barrier – for example, one is on a higher level or stands the
  other side of a stack of chairs.
- They then go into Repetition.

This is a useful exercise for creating connection between actors in a
scene where they need to be physically separated. For example, in
Romeo and Juliet 2.2, Shakespeare has set up a barrier between the
two characters with Juliet on her balcony and Romeo standing
below her in the Capulet orchard. Observers of this exercise may
notice how the actors' volume and tone of voice are affected by the

separation and how the intensity of the eye contact and responsiveness can increase when there is a restriction in place.

Summary of Repetition

- Repetition is an exercise fundamental to Meisner's technique. Its purpose is to establish connection with another actor, through actively listening and repeating what they say.
- Two actors connect with each other and repeat simple phrases about what they observe in the other person moment to moment.
- Repetition focuses on impulses rather than the words.
- Once you've learned the basic exercise, it can be used flexibly and with various given circumstances.

5

Independent Activity and Knock on the Door

Everything in acting is a kind of heightened, intensified
reality – but it's based on justified reality.

SANFORD MEISNER (1987: 45)

Once his actors were comfortable with Repetition, Meisner brought
in the concept of the Independent Activity. In this exercise an actor sets
up a task that is difficult but achievable and which aims for an
outcome that is important to them. Meisner's example is to give one
student (Vince), a name 'K. Z. Smith' to find in a Manhattan telephone
directory; with the plausible story that Vince has lost the number Ms
Smith gave him but wants to see her again. As Vince becomes absorbed
in searching through the pages of Smiths in the directory, another
student approaches him and begins Repetition ('Looking for
something?' / 'I'm looking for something'). This creates different
instinctive responses through the real tensions for Vince as he tries
both to focus on his task and to respond to his partner using Repetition.

Creating an Independent Activity

Meisner (1987: 39) asks all his students 'to choose something to do
which is above all difficult, if not almost impossible' and insists they
must have a clear reason why they want to do it, 'because that's the
source of your concentration and eventually of your emotion'. The
key elements of the Independent Activity are that it must be:

1   difficult, if not almost impossible, to carry out; and
2   important to you, in that there is a personally important
     reason for you to want to do it.

In the example activity that Meisner (1987: 39) gives Vince, the common surname makes the task hard but not impossible, and requires Vince to concentrate in order to have any chance of achieving it. Achieving the task becomes his objective. The incentive to achieve it is the opportunity to meet up with the attractive woman again, which then provides the stakes for achieving this objective. As Vince puts it, if he doesn't find the phone number, he will 'spend Saturday night alone'. This gives him a strong, imaginary but highly plausible incentive to succeed, which is grounded in reality. Vince can feel a realistic entitlement to believe he should succeed because the woman gave him her number and so wants him to call her; he just needs to overcome the obstacle of having lost the paper she gave him.

The key to a truthful performance for Meisner was that the actor has a personal, realistic connection to their actions. Plausibility is crucial. When another student offers an Independent Activity of completing a wooden puzzle because if he does he will win a million dollars, Meisner suggests he reduce the potential winnings to a thousand dollars so that it feels more within the realms of a realistic prize. Meisner continually emphasizes the importance of keeping both the activity and the reason to achieve it as simple as possible. Another of his students gives herself a complicated backstory of volunteering at a hospital for children with cancer and supporting a particular child to learn Shakespeare passages that she has on a set of cards because the child dreams of being an actor. Meisner (1987: 105) cuts her story short, telling her, 'It's too complicated.' Instead they agree she wants to learn how to make a house of cards in order to distract the child from his situation. Meisner explains that the complexity of her story would result in too much complexity of thought and feeling to connect her to the emotional reaction she is trying to achieve. He says, 'You can get more involvement for yourself by knowing that you're doing it to entertain a dying child. Simplicity is essential. Don't clutter yourself.' Plausibility and simplicity are crucial for this exercise because the complexity of the text will then be layered on top of it.

Knock on the Door

Meisner added a further element to the exercise of one actor setting up in an Independent Activity and a second engaging them in Repetition as outlined above. This further element is that the second actor knocks on a door before entering. This knock interrupts the first actor's focused activity and they must answer the knock with an instinctive response. Their first response may be verbal or non-verbal but it should be a genuine response to the moment which stems from their own feelings of being engaged in their activity and the quality of the knock. The actors then progress the scene through Repetition.

For example, the first actor might open the door either making or avoiding eye contact and begin the Repetition with the line 'You knocked.' Their partner responds 'I knocked' and perhaps follows the first actor as they return to their activity. The first actor's next response 'You knocked' may be said quizzically, angrily, indifferently or in many other ways, coloured by how that actor feels in that moment. The Repetition may begin with or may change at any time to a different observation, 'You're writing', 'You're wearing a blue jumper', 'You're smiling', even just 'You're there.'

Both actors continue the scene using Repetition as the words they speak in response to each other's actions and attitudes. Meisner explains that any knock will carry a meaning through how it is done: maybe timid, maybe nervous, maybe angry, maybe playful. The first actor's job is to respond to that meaning in that moment. They may hesitate at first, not wanting to open the door, or they may leap up immediately. They should answer the door in the way they feel they need to in that moment. Both actors then respond to each other on instinct as they repeat lines, based on what their partner does.

As a next stage to this exercise, Meisner (1987: 57) asks the actor knocking to have a reason to come in: 'And the reason has to be simple and specific and not death-defying in its urgency' – something like borrowing sugar from a neighbour. This reason should not become what the scene is about, but simply roots the actor in a reality.

The key elements of the Independent Activity are about stimulating the imagination and allowing the actor to fully commit to that fantasy situation. Within the imagined situation the actor has something simple but difficult that they are trying to achieve, and a clear, plausible and personal reason for trying to achieve it.

When the exercise is combined with Knock on the Door, the second actor presents an obstacle in the way of the first actor achieving their objective. As the scene proceeds through Repetition, an audience can watch the tensions unfolding caused by this conflict. The task has to be done and responding through Repetition to another human being has to be done. The sense of purpose of the Independent Activity gives the actor stakes.

Doing nothing

In setting up the Independent Activity exercise, Meisner introduces a key tenet of his technique which has become subject to differences of opinion amongst his disciples: 'Don't do anything until something happens to make you do it' (1987: 40). He gives the instruction that rather than keep repeating, one actor can pause, if that feels the right thing to do, until something their partner does creates an instinct to speak again. He explains (1987: 42) that 'Acting is not talking. It is living off the other fellow.' By 'living' he means responding to the meaning that emerges from the other fellow's behaviour – how they speak and what they do, rather than the words they say. This instruction has become controversial because it can be taken as an excuse for an actor to blame another actor for not giving them anything to respond to. This attitude can be more to do with the actor's own anxieties about listening to their impulses than the reality of the situation. Meisner (1987: 142) was clear that the only thing you cannot do is nothing. Because all your instincts are at work assessing and interpreting your situation in every moment, any pause should be suffused with a need to pause rather than simply waiting for something to happen.

Exercise 1: Independent Activity with Knock on the Door

- Actor A goes outside the room and waits. Actor B is inside the room getting ready to do their Independent Activity.
- Actor B should have prepared an activity that is difficult to do and has importance to them. They set up any equipment required in an appropriate space in the room. For example, if you are mending the pieces of a broken jug, do you need a

table? Do you need to be near the lit window to try to see clearly? Do you have the right glue nearby?

- Once all their equipment is ready, Actor B considers their imaginary high-stakes situation. What is at stake if they fail? For example, is it their mother's favourite jug that they need to repair – perhaps a family heirloom that they borrowed without telling her?

- Actor B sets a timer. This should be the time they could reasonably get the task done in, if they were left in peace. It needs to be a time frame that is believable. They then begin their activity.

- Actor A, still outside the room, is signalled to begin their preparation. They are imagining something that puts them into an emotional state. For example, they may be considering an imaginary slight that makes them feel annoyed. Note the imaginary scenario should not necessarily implicate the person inside the room.

- Actor A then proceeds to knock on the door. Because they are under the influence of the imaginary 'annoyed' state, the knock may be short and sharp. They then need to respond to whether it is answered immediately or not and allow that to affect them – they might immediately knock again.

- Inside the room, Actor B is interrupted by the knock. They have to follow their impulses about this, so they either open the door or keep going with their activity. Eventually they answer and once the door is opened, they make the first call which is a response to the knock, 'That was a loud knock' which gets repeated by Actor A, 'That was a loud knock', responding with how they feel.

- The exercise continues, repeating or changing calls as usual. Actor A is only responsible for doing Repetition. Actor B obviously needs to continue with their activity but also has to repeat.

What emerges is how torn Actor B is and you can really see observing how the pressure of the stake causes problems. For example, sometimes the first piece hasn't even been glued together when the knock happens. Actor A may try and help or they might hinder the activity. Many a carefully placed card tower is blown to the ground when the person coming in has felt ignored. The moment-to-moment pressures of the Independent Activity failing or succeeding as the clock counts down and indeed the pressures created by the connection between the two actors under these circumstances transforms the Repetition into a dramatic event and helps train all the muscles needed for acting under imaginary circumstances that plays demand.

Exercise 2: *Two Gentlemen of Verona* (1.2)

Actor A and Actor B now take on the roles of Lucetta and Julia in this scene from *Two Gentlemen of Verona*. Julia, the lady of the house, has just been given a letter by Lucetta her maid who knows it's from Proteus, a boy that Julia likes. Julia doesn't want Lucetta to know just how much she likes him so she rips the letter up into little pieces.

JULIA

> This babble shall not henceforth trouble me;
> Here is a coil with protestation. [*Tears the letter.*]
> Go, get you gone, and let the papers lie.
> You would be fingering them to anger me.

LUCETTA

> She makes it strange, but she would be best pleased
> To be so angered with another letter. [*Exit.*]

The pieces of the letter are now effectively the 'equipment' needed to do the Independent Activity. The activity will be to try to put the pieces of the letter together just like the broken jug above. Julia's attention is fully deployed, as the activity is 'difficult to do', as the letter is in little pieces. There is a time imperative as the wind is blowing and it might all just get blown away. It really 'matters to her' as she is in love with Proteus and this is a love letter from him, so every word really counts.

JULIA

> Nay, would I were so angered with the same.
> O hateful hands, to tear such loving words!

Injurious wasps, to feed on such sweet honey
And kill the bees that yield it with your stings!
I'll kiss each several paper for amends.
Look, here is writ kind Julia. Unkind Julia!
As in revenge of thy ingratitude,
I throw thy name against the bruising stones,
Trampling contemptuously on thy disdain.
And here is writ love-wounded Proteus.
Poor wounded name, my bosom as a bed
Shall lodge thee till thy wound be throughly healed;
And thus I search it with a sovereign kiss.
But twice or thrice was Proteus written down.
Be calm, good wind, blow not a word away
Till I have found each letter in the letter,
Except mine own name. That, some whirlwind bear
Unto a ragged, fearful, hanging rock,
And throw it thence into the raging sea.
Lo, here in one line is his name twice writ,
Poor forlorn Proteus, passionate Proteus,
To the sweet Julia – that I'll tear away;
And yet I will not, sith so prettily
He couples it to his complaining names.
Thus will I fold them, one upon another;
Now kiss, embrace, contend, do what you will.

Lucetta unexpectedly re-enters the scene. She can be full of an indignant preparation considering their argument. Or perhaps she re-enters feeling conciliatory. Lucetta has to respond to behaviour from Julia that she might not have expected to see, which she must allow to affect her in that moment. Julia has to respond to her while still trying to salvage the letter but without looking like she is doing just that.

[*Enter* LUCETTA.]

LUCETTA
Madam, dinner is ready, and your father stays.

JULIA
Well, let us go.

LUCETTA
What, shall these papers lie like tell-tales here?

JULIA
If you respect them, best to take them up.

LUCETTA
Nay, I was taken up for laying them down.
Yet here they shall not lie, for catching cold.
[*Picks up pieces of the letter.*]

At this moment Lucetta can choose whether she will help or hinder Julia in her task.

JULIA
I see you have a month's mind to them.

LUCETTA
Ay, madam, you may say what sights you see;
I see things too, although you judge I wink.

JULIA
Come, come, will't please you go?

Another example of where this exercise can be useful is *The Tempest* 3.1, the 'log scene' where Ferdinand has been ordered by Prospero to move magically enhanced heavy logs as a punishment. Ferdinand discusses with himself and the audience his dilemma as he tries to move the logs and Miranda watches him secretly and then interrupts suddenly. It is very valuable to have the actor playing Ferdinand try to move something actually heavy, so, while observing health and safety, they could try to move a piano or some stacked chairs while speaking in order to really feel the weight and the struggle that would cause. When Miranda enters to speak to him (effectively the Knock on the Door), how will her responses and desire to help him affect how he tries to complete his Activity?

MIRANDA
If you'll sit down,
I'll bear your logs the while: pray, give me that;
I'll carry it to the pile.

FERDINAND
 No, precious creature;
 I had rather crack my sinews, break my back,
 Than you should such dishonour undergo,
 While I sit lazy by.

Ferdinand needs to achieve his almost impossible but important task, yet is also torn as he wants to speak to the woman he's just fallen in love with. Miranda wants to make the most of her time alone with him.

In addition to actions in the text, directors may also create an activity during a scene, for example, a character changing clothes, or having their hair done, such as the Nurse helping Juliet to prepare for the Capulet ball in *Romeo and Juliet* 1.3.

Summary of the Independent Activity

- An Independent Activity is a simple and plausible physical task that an actor tries to complete – for example, searching for a name or mending a broken object.
- The task needs to be difficult, if not almost impossible, to complete.
- The actor should find a personally important reason for wanting to complete the activity so that it matters to them.
- If the actor is fully engaged in the Reality of Doing as they try to get the task done, watching the actor's struggle draws in the observers.
- As an exercise, the Independent Activity stimulates the imagination and allows the actor to commit fully to their fantasy situation.

Summary of Knock on the Door

- Knock on the Door is an addition to the Independent Activity that brings a second actor into the exercise.

- While the first actor is engaged in trying to complete their task, the second actor interrupts that activity by knocking on the door.
- The knock itself should reflect the intention of the actor who is knocking. The knock becomes the instigating moment of the interaction, with the first actor responding truthfully on hearing the knock.
- When the first actor has answered the knock, the scene proceeds using Repetition as the first actor continues to try to complete their Independent Activity.
- This exercise allows the first actor to experience being under pressure as they need to keep up the Repetition and complete their task.

6

Given and imaginary circumstances

The life of the actor must not annihilate the deeper implications of the play which the playwright has written.

SANFORD MEISNER (1987: 191)

The final chapter of Meisner and Longwell's book *On Acting* records the discussions between Meisner and his students as they explore scenes from mainly contemporary plays. The chapter is entitled 'Final Scenes: "Instead of *merely* the truth"', and the quotation comes from Meisner (1987: 210 italics original) explaining that working with a play text means moving beyond living truthfully under the given but imaginary circumstances of an improvised exercise, and becomes about living truthfully under the given circumstances of the text. He says, 'Now we're beginning to edge up on the problem of playing the part.' One of his students clarifies this as 'We're not only bringing truth to it. We're also doing something specifically dictated by the character and the circumstances.' Another student offers, 'We're supposed to look at character instead of . . .' and Meisner completes her sentence with 'Instead of *merely* the truth'. Meisner is not suggesting the truth is in any way inconsequential when playing a role; it is instead the absolute bedrock of any performance upon which a character can then be built. The structure of the house which the actor must then inhabit is constructed from the materials of the given circumstances in the play, furnished by the interpretive choices that the actor and director make.

Meisner's key requirement is always that his actors live truthfully under the given or imaginary circumstances of the text. Although he often used the terms 'imaginary' and 'given' interchangeably, it is perhaps more helpful to define given circumstances as any information we are given by a playwright about a character taken from something they say themselves or something said about them in the play text, with imaginary circumstances as additional interpretive details from the actor's and director's imagination. Imaginary circumstances are then the personal imaginative connections the actor makes to be able to live truthfully under the given circumstances of the text. The actor must commit to these circumstances in order to see the world through the eyes of their character. Most importantly, all actors in a performance must fully commit to the sum of given and imaginary circumstances agreed by a company so that a coherent world can be created for the production.

Connecting to the given circumstances

In looking for the given circumstances of a text, Meisner was following Stanislavsky's process of examining the 'external circumstances' of what a playwright gives us in terms of facts and forms. The approach requires an actor to live in their character's present in order to fully breathe life into that character, although the actor should feel, as Stanislavsky (1981: 16) describes, 'that he has the past of his role behind him', along with 'a prospect of the future, dreams of it, guesses and hints about it'. In working on scenes, Meisner hotseats his actors to support them in uncovering and understanding the details of the circumstances of their character; pushing them to respond to his questions in the first person to find reasons and desires for their words and behaviours (1987: 216–17; 224–5).

In order to view the world, everything and everyone in it through the eyes of your character, you need to build their point of view and connect how, why and what they see to your own point of view on life. In Meisner's words (1987: 178), 'The first thing you have to do with a text is find yourself.' The basic information you need to build your character's point of view is in the text. Initially you are seeking out 'facts' within the world of the play, mining the text for any details about your character and noting them down. As you uncover everything your character knows and does, you build evidence that helps you see through the eyes of the character and begin to understand their needs and how something that happens to them affects them.

Meisner asked his students to note 'What is the character literally doing' line by line without interpretation, and to consider 'What is the need of the character in this scene?' Scott Williams interprets this 'need' not as an objective but as 'What is the fire in the belly?' In addition to Meisner's questions, Williams asks his students to note line by line, without embellishments or interpretations, 'What is the knowledge of your character before the scene begins?' Compiling these lists and notes becomes a process personal to the actor as they not only outline the 'factual' given circumstances for each scene but begin to add their own interpretive and imaginary connections to complement and complete the circumstances the actor will play under.

These lists become very useful to the actor when you allow the knowledge to matter genuinely to you. You have to find yourself in that knowledge and give it personal meaning in order to live in your character's world. Bernardin describes the value of this work as follows: 'In order to understand what choices I need to make as an actor, I first need to understand both the commonality and difference between me and the character I'm playing.' Once you have clear lists of what your character does and knows, you can consider what the gaps are between the character and yourself. If you are playing Rosalind in As You Like It, for example, you consider whether you have a cousin or sister you are close to and draw from those feelings to connect to how Rosalind feels about Celia. If you have no such cousin or sister, however, your substitution might be your best friend, or even a best friend from school that you hardly ever see now but would still do anything for.

Sometimes connections can't be easily found. For example if you are playing King Duncan in Macbeth there is an obvious gap in that you are not a king. You can, however, look at the elements of being a king that might be important for the play and research royalty and politics to find out more about the attitudes and experiences you are looking for. Perhaps you need to find parallels for the sense of responsibility, of giving orders and being obeyed. You would then look at elements of your own life where you have experienced those things. Looking after small children can give you a sense of your power and their dependence, so maybe you can draw from your experience of being a parent, older sibling or babysitter. You can consider times when you have had to make decisions that seem necessary but not always popular, maybe in your professional or family life. In all of this, you are trying to align yourself to the point of view of your character and how they might see the world, finding parallel feelings in yourself for what you imagine they feel. You can then describe Duncan's situation to yourself by saying it is *as if* I am responsible for that group of children, or for my family, or this company of actors.

You can think about how these personal connections make you feel by considering Meisner's key metaphor of 'pinch and ouch' (outlined in Chapter 3). The 'pinch' comes from how you feel in response to the person or situation you are imagining, and the 'ouch' is how you respond in that moment under those imaginary circumstances. Inhabiting your character's world by making it mean something to you is a key part of a Meisner process. It is what Meisner (1987: 84) described as 'daydreaming', and allows insights from your imaginative connections with the text to subconsciously percolate and affect how you play a scene. These connections can emerge from quite a free association. Once you have your lists of knowledge about your character, created from the textual analysis work of mining the text for what your character knows and does, then you can talk around their situations and relationships in terms of status, affection, aversion and so forth. You will know when a connection feels right and invariably, as you discuss the character, you will suddenly say, 'Ah, I've got a link that makes sense.' These imaginative connections begin to build your imaginary circumstances to add to the given circumstances you have uncovered in the text.

Stage directions

In mining the text for information about a character, stage directions written by the playwright can seem useful. Meisner (1987: 191), however, encouraged his students to cross out any stage directions that interpret a character's behaviour; anything describing, for example, that they should speak 'softly' or 'angrily'. He explains such words 'are aids for *readers* of plays not for *actors* of them' (italics original). Actors need the freedom to find the spontaneous life of a character but, Meisner warns, within reasonable understanding of the intentions of the play.

With Shakespeare, descriptions of characters' behaviour, appearance and actions are almost always in the text as other characters' observations, rather than as separate stage directions. Olivia in *Twelfth Night*, for example, describes the 'contempt and scorn' she observes in 'Cesario', while Viola, disguised as Cesario, describes Olivia as 'too proud' but also 'fair' (*TN* 1.5). Such descriptions are details of the given circumstances of the play and have to be taken into account in playing the scene. Working with actors, a director may choose to change or ignore such descriptions, which is an interpretive choice any company is free to make, but it is worth considering how those changes affect the rest of the given circumstances.

Other given circumstances are in the implied action or conflict of the scene. In *Twelfth Night* 2.5, Malvolio cannot catch Sir Toby, Sir Andrew and Fabian hiding as he reads their prank letter. But if he *nearly* catches them it has great comedic value. Malvolio reads, 'If this fall into thy hand, revolve' (*TN* 2.5.140). He may see this as an actual instruction from Olivia, and ever dutiful turns around. If this is the exact moment that the trio are right behind him, they have to move fast so as not to get caught. The given circumstance that the trio cannot be caught out is what makes the scene dramatically successful. Choreographing this scene becomes like a dance with beats and key fixed specific moments.

Acting as intuition

For Meisner, acting is about learning to 'funnel instincts', training yourself to understand your instinctive emotional responses through key exercises like Repetition in order to be ready to respond on impulse when performing. Intuition, instinct and impulse are often used synonymously to suggest how someone has an immediate, unconscious understanding of a situation, a 'gut' response to what is right. Meisner (1987: 185) suggests, however, that such a response in the realm of acting is the result of hard work, life experience and talent. This is more a description of intuition, as psychologists are increasingly understanding it, rather than instinct or impulse. Intuition is better thought of as a shortcut to the store of accumulated knowledge in our long-term memories, often felt in the gut. When a firefighter, pilot or health care professional is faced with a burning building, engine malfunction or sick child, they subconsciously pick up cues about that particular situation, compare it with similar situations from past experiences, whether real or imagined through training, and respond accordingly. What feels like instinct comes from the patterns and associations their brains have previously observed and learned. They have learned how to operate effectively, efficiently and subconsciously under a set of given circumstances.

Intuition only becomes reliable through practice and feedback. The example most of us can relate to is learning to drive. While we are learning, there seems a huge amount of information to absorb: how a car behaves; the rules of the road; the dynamics of traffic. Eventually, all this learning becomes second nature and we drive intuitively. Just like learning to drive, any expert learns the processes and techniques associated with their craft. Actors learn how to work with text, voice, movement, design, the director's vision and technical requirements, and rehearsals give them practice and feedback.

If rehearsals are not just about doing a scene again and again until you have learned a repeatable pattern to perform, but about exploring possible differences each time you repeat the scene, as other experts in their fields do, then you learn about the world you are inhabiting. With our driving analogy, you might think about a new production as driving around a new area: you apply your skills of driving and learn the best routes and rhythms of the local traffic, but you have to remain constantly alert and responsive moment to moment to the behaviour of others. An actor's work throughout rehearsals is about getting this associative learning into your subconscious. You apply your skills to learning everything about the new area – the given circumstances of your character – then you are free to work intuitively, responding in the moment. All the given and imaginary circumstances you have worked on become the store of knowledge in your long-term memory. You can then draw from that to give you expert intuition in responding 'in character' to your fellow actors in every new moment.

Exercise 1: Creating a list of everything your character knows

Using the **third person**, write a list of **everything** your character **literally** knows **before** the **scene** starts and **add questions** for anything you want to examine further.

Third person – this is to avoid becoming attached to interpretive choices too early on.

Everything – all the information your character says about themselves or heard others say; all the people they have met and what they know about their relationships with those people.

Literally – no guessing, no imagining, only what is literal fact in the world of your character or what you think could reasonably be true but needs further examination. For example, it is reasonable to assume Lady Macbeth has given birth, but you will have questions.

Before – not during. Not after.

Scene – the unit of analysis for this process, the scene, begins with the moment a character enters, and ends at the moment a character exits.

Add questions – these are *your* questions prompted by whatever is not immediately or entirely obvious from the text.

Example: Lady Macbeth

Knows before her first entrance in 1.5:

She is a woman.

She is married to Macbeth. *For how long?*

She once had a child who died? *True? When? How old? How long ago?*

She has no other children? *True?*

She knows Macduff. *Has she met him before?*

She knows Banquo is Macbeth's good friend. *Has she met him?*

She knows King Duncan. *Has she met him?*

She knows Lady Macduff? *True? Met her before?*

She knows Macbeth is Thane of Glamis. *How long for? How hard won? Low or high title?*

He's away fighting the Norwegian army. *How long has he been away?*

Knows he's sent a message. *She hasn't read it yet – or has she?*
Malcolm and Donalbain are the king's sons. *Has she met them?*
Knows the likely line of succession.
Knows that kings are believed to be God on earth (if the play is set
    in Shakespeare's time with a belief in the Great Chain of Being).

Your first list will always be the longest. As you go through the play,
you add to it as you gain more knowledge. For Lady Macbeth's
second entrance, you should add everything she now knows from
her first scene and anything factual that's happened before her
second entrance, and so on in subsequent scenes.

Knows before 1.6:
Everything on the above list plus:

Macbeth has come home.
Knows they had a moment together.
Macbeth has been made Thane of Cawdor unexpectedly.
Macbeth and Banquo met three witches whose prophecy
    immediately came true about Macbeth becoming Thane of
    Cawdor. *What does she believe about witches?*
Knows the other prophecy about him being King. *Does she want to
    be queen?*
Knows she's called on the spirits to help her kill King Duncan by
    making her 'strong'. *Has she summoned them before?*
Knows she's discussed a plan with Macbeth to kill King Duncan
    that night. *Have they discussed logistics?*
She's told her messenger to look after the other messenger. *How
    much does she trust the messenger?*
She's got the house ready for the arrival of King Duncan. There's no
    time to prepare properly.
She's told Macbeth to look the part of an innocent host. *Does she
    know he is good at faking or not?*
King Duncan and his entourage are due to arrive imminently.

Knows before 1.7:
Everything on the above list plus:

Duncan's entourage has arrived and Lady Macbeth has greeted
    them.

She knows they are all having a banquet to celebrate the end of the war.

Macbeth has disappeared from the room. *How long has he been gone?*

She knows the King has asked where he is. *Is that true?*

Look at the first two lines as she enters the room:

MACBETH
   Hath he ask'd for me?

LADY MACBETH   Know you not, he has?

Mac 1.7.30

This is a good example of something to interrogate further. Lady Macbeth's response, 'Know you not he has', does not necessarily mean it is a fact that Duncan has asked for him. She may have her own reasons for suggesting Duncan has said something he has not. If something a character says is not obviously true, you have a decision to make for your performance. Look to see if other characters corroborate what people say. Is the fact repeated? Do other facts back it up? If it isn't clearly a fact, then it becomes an interpretive choice to be made in consultation with the director. A directorial choice might make the decision for you – for example, can we hear in the background tankards banging tables as Macbeth's name is being chanted? Whatever you decide will have an impact on how you eventually play that moment. Uncover the facts, make choices as needed and leave all else to be discovered while rehearsing with your fellow actors.

Exercise 2: Creating a list of everything your character does

Using the third person, write a list of everything your character **literally does or says during the scene**, including their **speech**.

Literally – no assuming or imagining actions the character might do.

Does – include all stage directions written in a good edition like the Arden series and all actions implicit in the text.

During – not before. Not after.

Scene – a scene starts when a character enters and ends when they leave.

Speech – create a concise summary of everything your character says during the scene.

Example: Lady Macbeth
Does in 1.7:

She enters the place where her husband has gone to. *How long has she been looking for him?*

She asks her husband why he left the banquet. She discusses with her husband why he must go through with their plan to kill Duncan and how they should proceed to carry out their plans.

The result of these lists is that your personal discoveries begin to emerge as meanings suggest themselves to you and you can feel empowered that they are rooted in the facts of the play. Remember, however, that you now know *what* you are doing and saying, you do not know *how*, *why* or *when* you say anything. The answers to those questions only come when rehearsing with another actor.

Summary of given and imaginary circumstances

- Meisner uses the terms 'given' and 'imaginary' circumstances interchangeably to discuss the information that an actor uses to create their character's point of view.

- It can be useful to think of given circumstances as the 'facts' mined from the text about what a character does or says, including what other characters say about them. Imaginary circumstances are then the actor's imagined embellishments on those 'facts' based on their personal interpretations.

- Creating and interrogating character 'knowledge lists' is a useful way to assemble the facts, explore the writer's intentions and make personal connections to your character.
- This work allows you to develop intuitive responses built on knowledge.

7

Preparation and As Ifs

You know, learning to act takes time. It's made out of the human being who's doing the work.

SANFORD MEISNER (1987: 161)

Having established the exercises of Repetition, Independent Activity and Knock on the Door, Meisner worked with his actors on the concepts of Preparation and 'As Ifs'. Both Preparation and 'As Ifs' are about the actor engaging their imagination to get them into the right place emotionally to inhabit the scene. Meisner's distinction between them was:

- Preparation gets you into the right emotional state to *enter* the scene and can change depending on what you need in that moment to feel what you need to feel.

- 'As Ifs' provide the feeling another character induces in you *during* a scene. The 'As If' is your interpretation of 'what the moment is about emotionally' (Meisner, 1987: 140). 'As Ifs' are worked out in rehearsal and remain constant for that production.

What each of these emotional stimuli is depends on the personal imagination or 'daydreaming' of the actor, and actors should feel no pressure to share them. Meisner (1987: 85) follows Freud in suggesting that most fantasies are based on ambition or sex, which is why they are best kept private. He explains, 'The fantasy of the daydream is the most personal, most secret of the acting values' (1987: 89). When working with Shakespeare's text, Preparations and 'As Ifs' can be seen as ways to build the imaginary circumstances introduced in the last chapter based firmly in the given circumstances of the text found through creating the knowledge lists. They provide tangible personal connections to support the actor in inhabiting the emotional world of their character.

Preparation

Meisner (1987: 128) advises his actors, 'Don't come in from nowhere.' Working with the Knock on the Door exercise, he whispers an 'emotional circumstance' to the actor knocking, something that has just happened to her, so that she comes into the scene feeling angry. Her partner has to respond, through Repetition, to her behaviour without knowing what she is angry about while all the time wanting to return to his Independent Activity. This situation parallels real life when we respond to friends, family and colleagues without knowing what is behind the emotional state we perceive in them. Our responses in such situations may involve various tactics: we may try to calm them, block them, maybe provoke them. The tension created as the actors' Repetition responses bounce off each other in this situation becomes very engaging for an audience to watch, regardless of the meaningless text. Adding an emotional circumstance to the exercise, says Meisner, 'made it a scene' (1987: 71).

Meisner (1987: 84–5) describes Preparation as 'daydreaming' – a fantasy that emotionally affects the actor and something that each actor has to find in their own way. He explains (1987: 89), 'What it means in ordinary language is that we use our imagination in order to fulfill in ourselves what we have more or less determined is our emotional condition *before* we start the scene' (italics original). Meisner insists that an actor should never come in 'empty' but always with a full and forceful feeling engendered by a Preparation that is simple and specific, and makes sense for the given circumstances of whatever the scene requires. He offers Hamlet as an example: 'In the beginning of the play, Hamlet is in a deep depression. What causes it?' (1987: 103). His students offer the facts of the play: his father has met an untimely death and his mother has married his uncle. For Meisner, these are the given circumstances of the play that then require an actor to enter with a Preparation that fits those circumstances. In this case, the actor should find a simple but specific daydream that triggers for them a feeling that manifests as deep depression. They then bring this fullness of feeling to the first moment of the scene. That might mean imagining the personal reality suggested by those given circumstances, but it might mean another fitting imaginary circumstance is needed for an actor who perhaps never knew their father, or who does not have an uncle.

Preparation for Meisner (1987: 78) is 'that device which permits you to start your scene or play in a condition of emotional aliveness'. As a device, it is not necessarily about remembering something that *actually* happened to you. Where do you need to go in your imagination to find a comparable situation to Hamlet's? Maybe it is the death of a parent, but maybe you are deeply attached to your dog and can imagine how empty your life might feel if your dog were run over and no one else took your loss seriously. Once the daydream is in place, the Preparation can be triggered and adjusted by physical action. For example, before entering as Hamlet, you might crouch in a corner and tense all your muscles, or you might lean heavily against a wall with all your weight in your legs – whatever works best for you to physically trigger the feeling of 'depression' in your body that connects to the knowledge of the character in your mind. When a student asks what could be used as Preparation to speak Hamlet's 'Too, too solid flesh . . .' soliloquy, Meisner replies, 'I don't know . . . I don't know who's playing it' (1987: 104). He is underlining that Preparation has to be personal – one person's fantasy of the cause of deep depression will not be the same as someone else's.

Only for the first moment

Crucial also for Meisner (1987: 79) is that 'Preparation lasts only for the first moments of the scene, and then you never know what's going to happen'. You come into the scene with a personal feeling generated from what seems a suitable parallel for your character's feeling and then respond to whatever happens next. What you then experience in that moment of arrival into the scene is coloured by your prepared feeling. Meisner (1987: 80) gives as an example the nineteenth-century actor William Charles Macready, who he says 'used to try to shake the iron ladder backstage that was embedded in the brick' before going on as Shylock in *The Merchant of Venice*. Meisner explains, 'He'd try and try, and would get furious because he couldn't budge it. *Then* he went on and played the scene' (italics original).

Your Preparation gives you the first expression of emotion, and then you immediately shift your attention outwards, see your partner clearly and respond to them. That first moment leads on to the next, so you must not hold on to the feeling you entered with, but instead allow yourself to be open and responsive to the other actors and the audience in each moment. If you allow yourself to be affected by your fellow actors, your emotional state will organically change. In Meisner's (1987: 199) words, 'A Preparation is only for the *beginning* of the scene, and each moment feeds it and changes it.' It may be, however, that those changes are only small shifts and nuances, rather than big shifts in mood. Rehearsing a scene with his actors, Meisner (1987: 205) instructs one actor that her Preparation is 'I want to die because of what happened' and adds, 'But if you're in a condition where *you honestly want to die*, it doesn't last only for a minute, it goes on and on' (italics original).

Preparation connected to Meisner's exercise of Knock on the Door is a powerful rehearsal tool which colours the first moment, fully allowing the actor to be *ready* in a specific way that then springboards the whole scene. Working on a scene, you can take the first moment of eye contact as the equivalent of the Knock (see Chapter 11). There is a connection immediately and both actors, coming in with their Preparation, are emotionally alive to the moment. For example, your Hamlet may enter his first scene with a sense of depression coloured by irritation. He may make eye contact with Claudius, who looks him up and down. This might make you feel angry or self-protective, or it might shock you out of your irritation into laughing at him. It's important to allow your Preparation to colour your first moment but not to paint over it.

Choosing Preparations

Look at the given circumstances of the scene (see Chapter 6) to check what you know before the scene starts and consider how that might make you feel going into it. Next consider what your *expectation* is of what is going to happen in the scene. For example, if you are Goneril entering the first scene of *King Lear*, are you expecting to make a speech about how much you love your father, and does that make you feel anxious or excited? Or are you expecting just another meeting of the court where Cordelia gets all the attention as usual, which makes you feel bored or irritated? The Preparation you choose depends on the given circumstances of the text and your interpretation of how you feel about them. Meisner (1987: 128) told his students, 'Come in from some situation which has a circumstance in it that gives you a foothold for a Preparation.'

How you get into your Preparation can be anything that changes your everyday energy state so it matches what is required for the start of the scene. For example, if you the actor are running late and arrive at the theatre highly agitated and stressed, that might be a useful Preparation for Prince Escalus' first entrance in *Romeo and Juliet*, but is not the state of 'emotional aliveness' that Romeo needs for his entrance when he has been mournfully thinking of Rosalind. The Preparation shifts your real-life energy state before you play the scene.

Preparation exercise with Repetition

Once you have chosen what seems a good Preparation for a scene, you can test it with your scene partner by taking it into the Knock on the Door exercise outlined in Chapter 5. Use Repetition only at this stage in order to discover what might be happening underneath the words when coloured by your Preparation.

1 Actor A chooses a Preparation.
2 Actor A Knocks on the Door of a room where Actor B is simply waiting in order to do Repetition with them.
3 Actor B responds to the Knock, which is the first moment and has been coloured by Actor A's Preparation, and the Repetition begins. One actor begins by saying something aloud that they observe as being true of the other. The second repeats this line from their own point of view. Each actor can change the call according to the other person's shifting behaviour. For example: 'That was a loud knock' / 'That was a loud knock', 'You're frowning' / 'I'm frowning' . . .

The outside eye of the director is important here. As a director, you can check whether a Preparation is colouring the actor in the 'right' way for your vision and ask them to adjust their Preparation for more of the emotion you feel is needed, without them needing to reveal to you how they will get to that emotion. For example, in *Romeo and Juliet* 3.1, Romeo enters to find Tybalt and Mercutio squaring up to fight. He has just secretly married Juliet and therefore a director might suggest to the actor a Preparation of feeling ecstatically happy about being in love. In the first moment, Romeo sees his friends about to fight with Juliet's family and cannot retain those happy feelings. Those feelings, however, now affect how the scene plays out. Romeo wants to believe that the universe wishes him and Juliet to be together, and so far he has 'learned' that this is true – everything has gone well so far. He proceeds accordingly, trying to make peace through actions that the audience can recognize as mere wishful thinking. The actor's Preparation for this scene has made them see through love-tinted glasses. If, as a director, you decide Romeo has too much energy at the start and you would like him to be slower in his thinking, adjust the Preparation. Rather than being in love and happy, Romeo could use a Preparation which is more in love and bewildered. Making small adjustments like this can have a big effect on the scene.

As Ifs

'As Ifs' are central to Meisner's process as ways for an actor to inhabit a character's situation with their own emotional imagination. He took this idea from Stanislavsky's concept of particularization. In this quotation, Meisner is encouraging a student to find her personal link to the given circumstance in the text that the man she loves is leaving her because he believes her to be a lesbian:

> To him a lesbian is an appalling pervert, but his accusation touches off nothing emotional in you. It's just words on paper, a cold text. How do you solve this problem? In this case, let's say that this is *as if* you were accused of something which is horrifying to you. Now I don't know what's horrifying to you, but if you're honest with yourself, you'll find something in your experience or imagination (1987: 137)

Meisner tells his student that she needs to find something real *for her* to fill this gap in feeling between her own reaction and her character's; otherwise she is sounding sad but with no real depth or truth beneath her words. He tells his class, 'This is where the *as if* comes in. It's pure Stanislavsky. It's *as if* she were a five year old and something dreadful happened to her – something miserable, something degrading' (1987: 137, italics original).

Meisner (1987: 139–40) explains how you can find an emotional parallel for your character's situation that allows you to emotionally inhabit the moment, even though you may well have no experience of such a situation. He gives the example of two actors cast as football players: one player is badly hurt and the other is waiting for help. Meisner suggests that as a director he might say, 'Stand there and watch him *as if* he were your wife who is dying.' He goes on, 'Now, God knows that has little to do with two football players, but we, the audience, will never know where you got your emotion, although we will be responsive to it.' The audience picks up on the actor's feeling and because this feeling is framed by the situation in the play, they apply it to that context: 'The audience attaches the emotion to what he's doing.'

Following Meisner's principles of finding connection between actors or 'living off the other fellow', 'As Ifs' are most usefully applied to other people. We speak, react and behave differently with different people and in different situations. Consider, for example, how you speak in front of your grandmother compared with your friends. You may swear around your friends unthinkingly but probably never swear around your grandmother. You don't choose not to swear, you unthinkingly never do it because that is part of the habitual pattern of behaviour that makes you behave differently with her. So, if your 'As If' on the other actor is your grandmother, you intuitively know how to behave. Not just your choice of language, but also your body language, voice and eye contact can all unconsciously change. We can tap into this everyday unconscious, habitual behaviour to help us find emotional truth in a moment with another actor. In a scene, you would say it's 'As If' the other actor is my mother-in-law or 'As If' they're a naughty child. Essentially it is substituting someone, or something you know, or can imagine, for the person (or thing or situation) in front of you.

An important aspect of an 'As If' is whether it gives or takes away permission. Ask yourself: who gives you permission to be yourself? Your best friend, your brother, your girlfriend? Who takes away your permission to be yourself? The police, your mother, your boss, your ex-boyfriend? If you change who you see, that person's behaviour is now entirely coloured by who you are imagining them to be. If, as Hamlet, you see Claudius as your strict Maths teacher who always made you feel stupid, you will respond differently to him than if you see him as your boss who was generally incompetent.

Choosing As Ifs

Stand outside your character and evaluate whom they are talking to in a scene. Consider: what status does this character have, relative to mine? For example, if you are playing older than a fellow actor, 'As If' them as someone younger. If a link is clear, you do not need to make up something. There's no point, for example, searching for an 'As If' on an actor as someone you fancy if you already do fancy them; remember you don't need to tell anyone what your 'As If' is. Actors should not share their 'As Ifs' out loud. If everyone knows this information will remain private, they can feel free to use the most powerful substitute they can imagine without feeling ashamed or worrying about giving offence or being exposed.

'As Ifs' as authority figures – police officers, for instance – can make actors incredibly wary. They may shut down or lose eye contact, their body language gets defensive and they become tense and overly polite. Remember, however, that the 'As If' is subjective and unique. If your sister is a police officer, you will have an entirely different point of view of the police than someone who has been stopped by the police multiple times. If your 'As If' is an 'old person' whom you don't know, you might speak louder, repeat yourself or be overly kind and patient. If it is your neighbour who is always rude to you, you might be less patient. Using best friends for 'As Ifs' allows you to interrupt more and be much louder. Facing 'nuns' and 'priests' can cause an unconscious covering of genitals. As with Preparation, testing your 'As If' with Repetition is the most efficient way of seeing if you're in the right territory for the scene. If it's wrong, adjust or change the 'As If' and discover what happens.

Exercise 1: Repetition with Preparation and As Ifs

1 Set up Repetition with both actors having a secret 'As If' on the other. The 'As If' can be given to them by a director (suggestions below).

2 Ask the actors to look down until told to look up. The exercise begins when both actors make eye contact.

3 One actor begins by saying something aloud that they observe as being true of the other. Once the 'As Ifs' are in place, whoever feels the most permission according to their status will tend to speak first. The second actor repeats this line from their own point of view. Each actor can change the call according to the other person's shifting behaviour. For example: 'You're smiling' / 'I'm smiling', 'You're smiling' / 'I'm smiling', 'You're laughing' / 'I'm laughing' . . .

4 After each round, share your discoveries. As an actor: how did the 'As If' affect your behaviour? As a director: how did you perceive the changes in behaviour? What narratives did you see emerging?

5 Add a Preparation that colours how you begin the Repetition. Discuss how this affects your scene.

6 Try out different 'As Ifs' and different Preparations to discover how different combinations work. Take turns in watching and performing.

7 Discuss how the feelings we bring to the scene affect our perceptions about someone else and how our different perceptions about people change our behaviours. Consider also how an outside eye reads those different behaviours.

Suggested 'As Ifs'
Mother-in-law
Police officer
A casting director

Person you fancy but have never told
An ex who you hurt
Your best friend

Partner who you've just found out has cheated on you
A colleague who you feel has been unfairly promoted over you
Someone you fancy who you saw kissing someone else

Your best friend's partner who is coming on to you and whom you
    fancy
A one night stand whom you have fallen in love with
The naughty child of your boss

Through this exercise you will notice how much a small gesture or
movement made by your partner affects you: an eyebrow raise, a
step back, a smile. You find yourself asking, why has my mother-in-
law just frowned or stepped back? For actors, this may feel like
suddenly you're 'in your head' and thinking too much, but once an
'As If' is in place, this inner monologue becomes valuable as you the
actor thinking from the point of view of your character.

Exercise 2: *Romeo and Juliet* (1.3)

Early in *Romeo and Juliet*, Lady Capulet discusses marriage with
her daughter, with Juliet's Nurse present. All the actors in the scene
will need 'As Ifs' on each other and also for any characters they talk
about. Each actor can have a different 'As If' on each character. For
example, the actors playing Lady Capulet, Juliet and the Nurse can
each have a different 'As If' on Paris because the 'As If' is created
from each character's point of view and each actor's imagination. It
is therefore important that these imaginary substitutions remain
private. Let's take Lady Capulet as an example:

- For Juliet – choose someone younger who should obey you
  – maybe a younger relative whom you struggle to talk to.
- For the Nurse – choose someone you are dependent on but
  who can also be a gossip – maybe a junior work colleague
  who doesn't stop talking and interfering.

- For Paris – choose someone whom you admire. Is he a successful younger man, or perhaps a gorgeous film star you have a crush on?

During the scene, Lady Capulet also talks about and hears about specific things. You will need to have made 'As If' connections to them all, as part of your Preparation. You need to have a point of view on each word referring to a place, event or object when you hear it and when you say it. That connection will then affect you in the moment. For example

- She says, 'ladies of esteem, Are made already mothers'. Is she feeling a loss of status beacuse of other marriages that are being arranged in Verona?
- She hears the Nurse refer to Mantua, 'you were then at Mantua'. How does Lady Capulet feel about Mantua? Does she have happy or sad memories of her time there?
- She hears the servant say, 'the guests are come'. Does she know or dread which ones they are? Do they always come early? 'supper served up' – is that a good or bad thing? 'my young lady asked for' – is that Paris who is asking?

Once you have noted all the instances of possible connections, you get to make a choice which ones are things you know about or have significance to you.

Other uses for As Ifs

Another unexpected use for 'As Ifs' is if you are working with an actor who is not responsive. For example, you are playing Juliet and your Romeo is not making eye contact with you; he's looking above your head or to the side or sometimes just at the audience. What do you do? If you respond truthfully, you may be jumping around trying to get his attention. Alternatively you could pick an 'As If' of someone you really fancy and you have overheard they fancy you but are feeling incredibly shy about it. So now every time they don't look at you, you perceive that as, 'Ah, he loves me so much he cannot look me in the eye.' And you respond accordingly.

Sometimes there are circumstances where an actor may need more permission. In *Twelfth Night*, for example, Olivia needs permission to unashamedly pursue 'Cesario'. The actor playing Olivia will obviously need an 'As If' on Cesario as someone she really fancies, but if it is also 'As If' she has overheard someone say 'Cesario' really fancies her but is very shy, she will keep pursuing 'Cesario' and see green lights to proceed even when Viola is actually trying to shut her down.

Preparation summary

- 'The purpose of Preparation is so that you do not come in emotionally empty' (Meisner, 1987: 78).

- Preparation uses the given circumstances in the text to decide how a character should feel as they enter a scene.

- In creating their Preparation, an actor searches their imagination for a relationship or situation that would give them a similar feeling to how they think their character feels on entering a scene. They create a daydream or fantasy focusing on how they would feel if it really happened.

- It can be useful to establish a physical trigger to get quickly back into the feeling induced by that daydream.

- Preparation should be released into the first moment of the scene. It should affect the actor as they enter the scene but they should then allow their fellow actors to affect how they feel in the next and each subsequent moment.

As If summary

- The 'As If' is your interpretation of 'what the moment is about emotionally' (Meisner, 1987: 140).

- The 'As If' uses the given circumstances in the text to colour how a character feels as they respond during a scene in relation to what they are seeing and hearing.

- In creating their 'As If', an actor searches their imagination for a relationship or situation that would give them a similar feeling to how they think their character feels about each relationship or situation.

- The 'As If' remains constant throughout the scene.
- 'As Ifs' are subjective and unique to each actor and should remain private.

PART TWO

Bringing in text

8

Learning lines

Speaking should be free to the moment.
CICELY BERRY (1987: 16)

The exercises of Repetition, Independent Activity and Knock on the Door, along with an exploration of the concepts of As Ifs and Preparation, explored in previous chapters, formed the basis of a first year of classes under Meisner's two-year programme. They are far from the sum of his teaching but they encompass the techniques and principles for which he is best known. Once he had established his foundational principles of connection with his students, the principles we have summarized as seeing clearly and responding honestly from your point of view, Meisner's teaching moved on to working with text in what Strandberg-Long (2018) describes as 'The elusive second year'. She calls it elusive because, while the activities of the first year are described verbatim by Longwell, the second year text work that builds on this foundation is not similarly recorded, and lives on only in the interpretations of Meisner's students and the adaptations of the teachers who follow him. The process of the second year involved overlaying active textual analysis on to the emotional core of the foundational work of the first year and used Stanislavsky's language of objectives and particularizations, or 'As Ifs'. Meisner regarded text analysis as the last stage of the process once connection between actors had been established, and saw it as a process which centres on the actor understanding clearly the given circumstances of their character. Again, he followed Stanislavsky in noting and examining a character's physical action in a scene – everything they do, according to the playwright's words (as explored in Chapter 6).

William Esper, who trained under Meisner in the early 1960s, has co-authored two books with his own former student Damon DiMarco. The first, *The Actor's Art and Craft*, explores the key Meisner activities described in previous chapters as the foundation for the actor of 'developing themselves into truthful acting instruments'. The second, *The Actor's Guide to Creating a Character* (2014), is based on that 'elusive second year' of Meisner's training, building on the actor's emotional core to interpret a role. Esper (2014: 5) explains, 'Sandy used to say the first year of training an actor is like putting money in the bank. The second year is about learning to spend that money wisely.' Previous chapters have explored how to get that emotional currency banked in the very bones of the Shakespearean actor so that when they come to working with the text, that wealth creates a sustainable security and structure for the actor to feel free in how they spend it. Throughout this book, we have offered interpretations of Meisner's exercises and principles for working with Shakespeare. It is worth noting, however, that his second year work with text has been even more subject to adaptation by practitioners than the first. (For a discussion of how other Meisner teachers in the UK have worked with these principles, and particularly their links with Stanislavsky, see Shirley, 2010: 207–12.)

Learning lines

Sooner or later every actor has to address learning their lines. It is fundamental to the job; as the famous Spencer Tracy quote says, 'Know your lines and don't bump into the furniture.' In actor training, however, it is given little attention and most people find their own way through trial and error. But lines have to be learnt, and how and when you do it can make a lot of difference to how you rehearse and eventually perform.

As a relatively early exercise in his teaching, following Repetition and Knock on the Door, Meisner asks his students to learn a section of dialogue '*without* meaning, *without* readings, *without* interpretation, *without* anything. Just learn the lines by rote, mechanically' (1987: 67, italics original). He then asks them to run the scene with their partner, speaking the words in just that completely uninflected way. Many of his students find this deeply uncomfortable, but the point he wants to illustrates is perhaps best explained by one of his students, who says, 'I felt that it's so raw and so untouched when we do it by rote that what we can add to it emotionally is unlimited because we are free of immediately insisting that it be read one way or another' (Meisner, 1987: 67).

For many actors, the process of learning lines is an organic association with their character's intentions at certain points of a play and a muscle memory of how and where they are at that moment of performance. Using Meisner techniques means being fully in the moment, responding to your fellow actors. If the lines you hold in your head have been learned with patterns of meaning and association, you cannot bring that level of freedom to your speaking of them. If, however, you can recite your lines without any sense of hesitation, you can fully trust yourself to be in the moment. Meisner (1987: 131) warns that 'when you have to start thinking about what the next line is, it breaks the flow of emotion'. If the lines are fully in your long-term memory and you have learned them neutrally, the set could fall down and those lines will still fall out of your mouth in the correct order. Most importantly, your fellow actors could do anything and those words will still come. You can then give them meaning in that moment under your given set of circumstances.

Some directors say they don't want lines learned by the first day of rehearsals, but that is usually because they fear they will be fighting fixed cadence and inflection. Some actors say they don't like overworking running lines because of fears of becoming stale. They quite rightly want their lines to sound fresh each time they speak, but achieving a feeling of being spontaneous and alive by not being on top of your lines can leave the rest of the company terrified. Being confidently off book with lines learned neutrally at the start of rehearsals gives everyone enormous freedom to really explore the text.

LEARN BEYOND LEARNING

My insight into the value of learning lines beyond learning came from a very unexpected source. It came when I was visiting my aunt and grandmother in Goa. My grandmother Sybil was ninety and had advanced Alzheimer's. She would sit still most of the day in a rocking chair with her eyes on a fixed point.

At seven o'clock every evening, the church bells in the village would ring out. Goa has a strong Catholic tradition and my family there are very strong in their beliefs. The bell is rung to mark the time for the Angelus prayer – a series of prayers usually followed by a recitation of the rosary. So my beloved grandmother, having sat in silence all day not moving, upon hearing the Angelus bell would stand up, steady as you like, and recite these very long complex prayers. Some bits are call and response, and my aunt would chime in with the other part. At the end my grandmother would sit back down and not speak till the next day. It was astounding to witness. I recognized that this was because she, from a very young age, had done this same activity every day of her life. Every day. It was a huge part of her muscle memory that when the bell rang at that time, those words automatically came flying out of her mouth. It occurred to me that she had learned those prayers 'beyond learning'.

As my grandmother demonstrated, rote learning is used in religious learning as a way of getting lines deep inside somebody's brain. Catholics learn the rosary, Muslims learn the Koran, Jews memorize sections of the Torah. Young people in school will often learn lines like this for exact quotes that they need for exams. Actors however, who are dependent on their lines to do their job, often resist doing it effectively, even though, as Butterfly actor Elliot Thomas explains, 'You wouldn't go on stage and be constantly checking that your hat is still there – the same is with how much you need to know your lines.'

Learning lines neutrally

There is no trick to learning lines beyond the simple grind of rote learning. Rote learning is a method of memorizing information through repetition and focuses on getting that information stored in the long-term memory. It is something we have probably all experienced in our school careers when we memorized facts and quotations for exams. Such rote learning is often criticized as a learning technique for not requiring any understanding of the information being stored, but in this case that is exactly what you are aiming for – securely stored patterns of sound without any in-depth reflection on how or what they mean. The repetition of rote learning embeds lines deep in your memory so that they are at your disposal when cued, just like the words of a nursery line or a prayer. The value of Meisner's advice (1987: 70) to avoid learning lines with any emotional cadence is clarified by one of his students as depriving you 'of any preconceived emotional associations, so that once you learn the text this way, the emotion will come out of what your partner is giving you'.

Learning lines from Shakespeare without attention to the tone and inflection that brings meaning can seem counter-intuitive. Particularly because the words and syntax are not always familiar, our brains immediately try to solve the puzzle to feel intellectually confident in understanding what our character says. In trying to let go of this need for control, it can be helpful to consider the difference between sense and meaning. When we read words, we cannot help but get a sense of them: the associations and memories they arouse in us, the feel, texture and colour of them; even words in a foreign language are suggestive in this way. When we speak or write to express ourselves to others, we try to funnel that sense into a meaning that we can share.

Shakespeare was particularly good at preserving the ambiguities of language, and that ambiguity is what allows space for the individual actor to fill that text with their own life. Rather than being 'cold' as Meisner describes, text pulses with all the warmth of colours and textures that the sense of the words suggest for you. Learning lines neutrally means learning lines without meaning, but not without sense. It means noticing the instinctive personal feelings and associations that might bubble up from the patterns and rhythms of words and allowing them to flow freely around you, until such time as you give the words meaning by speaking them with intention in response to a specific moment under a specific set of given circumstances.

Trying to distract your mind from finding meaning while learning lines can take close monitoring, patience and a great deal of self-compassion. It all becomes worthwhile, however, when you stand opposite another actor who also has their lines fully learnt. Then you can discover the flow together as the lines come out of your mouths and you can be unthinkingly responsive to the thoughts and feelings those patterns of sounds and images create in you (see

Chapter 12). Only then can you have 'the courage to live at the moment of speech' as Cicely Berry urged (1987: 19).

Awareness of rhythm

In Meisner's exercise using rote learning, he insisted on a 'mechanical' approach specifically including 'no iambic pentameter, nothing but the cold text' (1987: 67). Longwell (1987: 67) tells us that, by way of illustration, Meisner chants, 'To / be / or / not / to / be / that / is / the / question' as 'his hand taps the desk mechanically on each syllable'. All playwrights, however naturalistic their writing appears, craft their language with an awareness of the rhythms of speech and dialogue, and Meisner was well aware of this. While his exercise on mechanical rote learning is a valuable illustration of the emotional blank canvas that words can provide, it is not necessarily an exhortation to learn lines entirely in this strict way. In fact he qualifies himself (1987: 69) by explaining that lines should be learned 'in as unmeaningful and yet in as relaxed a way as you can, so that you'll be open to any influence that comes to you'. In other words, he says, 'Neutral and relaxed . . . Not firm and tense'. Meisner does not insist on mechanical rote learning at all times, but he does counsel neutrality with line learning. He explains, 'If you are neutral, you will achieve a kind of emotional flexibility' (1987: 69).

Rote learning relies on rhythms to lay down the patterns of data in long-term memory. Think of times tables, prayers, nursery rhymes and the more successful mnemonics, and you will find rhythms to the sound patterns. Think how easily song lyrics slip into your head without noticing because they are backed by rhythm. The rhythms underscoring Shakespeare's writing, particularly the verse lines, can support rote learning if your approach to using them remains neutral and relaxed.

As you gain more confidence with Shakespeare's texts, you intuitively pick up on variations in the stress patterns. Disturbances to the iambic pentameter invite interpretations of tone and inflection that provide interesting and useful support for actors, all of which can be discussed with the director. Less confident actors, however, should beware of either becoming 'stuck' in the 'de dum de dum' of the rhythm or ignoring any sense of the rhythm in aiming for naturalism. Working with the rhythms, as John Barton (2009: 37) emphasized, supports an actor in finding the balance of naturalistic speech and the heightened nature of Elizabethan drama. Learning verse lines as units is also very helpful in getting the words deep into your memory.

Finding the rhythm of prose lines is more difficult and many actors find Shakespeare's prose harder to learn because of this, but the more you can find the rhythms, the easier the lines will fall into your head, and the more easily you can respond to the innate sensations of the words in your performance. The comedy of Shakespeare's clowns is in the very rhythms of how they speak. The emotional connection of Shylock's 'Hath not a Jew eyes ...' and the lack of it in Brutus's ill-fated speech after killing Caesar are in the rhythms they use.

Once you have a familiarity with your lines and a good sense of their rhythm, try the following exercises to get the lines deeply into your memory without inflection:

Exercise 1: Uninflected line learning

Working alone:

- Speak the lines aloud in a robotic, monotone voice.
- Speak the lines going up and down your vocal scale randomly. This helps to break any patterns. Try using a different note on every syllable.
- Say one word at a time that builds up – this is particularly slow, but most effective at not getting stuck in a pattern – To, To be, To be or, To be or not, To be or not to, To be or not to be ...
- Do an activity like washing up, juggling, or press-ups while speaking lines – any activity that gets you moving around.

Exercise 2: Playing games that put you under pressure

Working with others, speak your lines uninflected while playing games such as:

- throwing a ball between two or more people in a random pattern;

- piggy in the middle; or
- tag.

Exercise 3: Confirming cues

Working with your scene partner(s), speak your lines uninflected following these instructions:

- Pass a cushion, bottle of water, or other object between you. Soft things are easier to grab hold of.
- Do not make eye contact as this will make you want to react to your partner – look past the other actor at a fixed point behind them.
- Grab the cushion on your cue and say your line. Do not *pass* the cushion, the aim is to *grab* on your cue. This also helps with pace later on.
- Keep the pressure on each other and don't leave any pauses, not even micro-pauses, unless there is a pause in the text, in which case leave a gap.
- Do not speak the lines fast, but grab the cushion fast.
- As before, try speaking the lines in a robotic way, then up and down the scale. If you can manage this a few times effortlessly, you can feel assured that your lines are securely in your head.
- Remember this exercise is not about finding a need to speak or about your character's relationship with another character, it is simply about developing the muscle memory response to speak on cue.

Summary of line learning

- In order to use Meisner's methods effectively with text, it is important to keep your full attention on the other actor, and therefore you need to know your lines.
- To get the most benefit from this technique, the lines need to be learned without inflection.

- Physical games and distractions are useful in putting you under pressure while learning lines

- Learning lines uninflected is hard but don't give up.

- There is no short cut to learning lines, but there are huge benefits to ensuring lines are deep in your long-term memory. You are then able to put your attention fully out on the other actor and everything that is around you. This gives you freedom of expression, increased playfulness and the ability to respond instinctively.

9

Paraphrasing, Breaking the Back and soliloquies

You have to know what you're saying means to you.

SANFORD MEISNER (1987: 146)

There is often a fear factor in working with Shakespeare's text that holds actors back from fully letting their performance be in response to the other actor. Often when it comes to acting, directing or teaching Shakespeare, we bring so much cultural baggage with us that our fears of tripping over it make that baggage a barrier to exploration and play. Meisner's techniques offer the Shakespearean actor increased confidence in taking risks to find truthful ways into inhabiting the text. This means not ignoring that cultural baggage, but opening it up to rummage around and make discoveries. Through his alter ego of Tortsov, Stanislavsky (1981: 119) tells his students to 'read and listen to everything, as many plays as possible, criticisms, commentaries, opinions', but he insists they keep an independence of thought and form their own opinions, adding, 'You must know how to be free.' It is perhaps this sense of informed freedom to respond in a moment that Meisner most adopted from Stanislavsky.

In any practice with Shakespeare, it is worth remembering that unlike more modern playwrights who can and have offered some guidance on the intentions inherent in their work, all we have of Shakespeare are the black marks on the page and a lot of other people's opinions about them. That is not to say that those opinions are not worth seeking out, or that there is not a wealth of highly useful knowledge about how and why Shakespeare used his words.

Reading and experience of such ideas, interpretations and accumulated knowledge should become part of the personal knowledge and understanding that any Shakespeare actor, director or teacher brings to their work, and Meisner did not suggest otherwise. It is, however, in the crucible of performance that a play finds meaning, as an actor fills the text with their own life and audiences read that performance from their own points of view. The most important thing to remember in working with Shakespeare is that the only right way to do Shakespeare is to find *your* way – find what the text means for you in a moment of response with another actor and you will communicate that to your audience. In this chapter, we look at making the text your own through two exercises: Paraphrasing and Breaking the Back. We also consider how the Meisner actor learns to respond in the moment to the audience, as well as their fellow actors, and how this is particularly useful for soliloquies.

Paraphrasing

In working with text, one approach Meisner used involved making the material your own through initially improvising the dialogue and gradually replacing that improvisation with more and more of the playwright's words until you are speaking only that text. The importance of this exercise is in achieving a clear understanding and deep ownership of everything you say so that you can feel free with that text in the moment of performance. This improvisation of the dialogue is a form of paraphrasing that is not about finding an approximate modern translation for a speech, but a parallel that puts the language into words *you* would say in *your* everyday life. It requires not only adjustments for your contemporary use of metaphors, colloquialisms and syntax, but also your thoughtful, personal connections to what those words might signify for you.

Because the foundational element of Meisner's technique is that your performance must always be in response to your fellow actors, paraphrasing is best done as a shared experience, so that the company discovers possibilities of meaning together, actively listening and supporting each other. It is worth noting that sometimes the actual text is what you would normally say. If so, say that. There's no need to search for alternative words if you don't need to.

Exercise 1: Paraphrasing for clarity and connection

1 Sit opposite each other.
2 Go slowly.
3 Start attempting to put things into your own words, what is most natural sounding to you. For example, if the character says, 'Good morrow', you might say, 'Good morning' or even 'Hiya'.
4 Use the actual text if you really would say just that.
5 If you are unsure what any words or phrases mean, refer to glossaries and editions of the text. It is worth consulting more than one as they may offer you interesting nuances of meaning.
6 Try to find more personally meaningful metaphors to replace the ones Shakespeare uses.
7 Find 'As Ifs' to help you better connect to the people, things and situations you are talking to and about (see chapter 7).

Example: *The Tempest* (3.1)

This is an example of how you might paraphrase this extract, but remember your version has to be in words *you* would use in your everyday life.

MIRANDA   Alas, now, pray you,
    Work not so hard. I would the lightning had
    Burnt up those logs that you are enjoined to pile!
    Pray set it down and rest you. When it burns,
    'Twill weep for having wearied you. My father
    Is hard at study; pray now, rest yourself.
    He's safe for these three hours.

                                    Tem 3.1.15–21

Paraphrase: Oh God, now please stop overworking. I wish lightning had set fire to those logs that you have been forced to pile up. Please put it down and rest. When it burns, the sap will ooze out like it's crying. My father (find an 'As If' for someone you respect and admire who would be furious if they knew were doing something they disapprove of) is really busy. Please rest. He won't come by for another three hours.

> FERDINAND   Admired Miranda!
>   Indeed the top of admiration, worth
>   What's dearest to the world! Full many a lady
>   I have eyed with best regard, and many a time
>   Th' harmony of their tongues hath into bondage
>   Brought my too diligent ear. For several virtues
>   Have I liked several women; never any
>   With so full soul but some defect in her
>   Did quarrel with the noblest grace she owed
>   And put it to the foil. But you, O you,
>   So perfect and so peerless
>
> *Tem* 3.1.37–48

Paraphrase: Amazing Miranda (find an 'As If' for Miranda – the greatest beauty you've ever seen or maybe someone famous). I have checked out many women (find an 'As If' for some beautiful women you know) and have spent loads of time hanging on their every word (find an 'As If' for a long flirty conversation). I've liked several women (find an 'As If' for women who are great but have issues) for their good qualities but something about them was always wrong. But you. Oh you are so perfect and beyond comparison.

The benefits of paraphrasing for actors

- Gaining confidence with the text.
- Recognizing how you have to 'new mint' words, discovering how to express something in the moment as if for the first time.
- Aligning you with the writer's struggle to search for expression. You discover how characters have to search for words to express themselves fully.

- Alerting you to any words that you may have skimmed over with a general understanding and ensuring you have a clear and personal understanding of every word.
- Helping you discover Shakespeare's specificity of word choice.
- Helping you expand your interpretive choices.

Breaking the Back

Don't pick up cues, pick up impulses.
SANFORD MEISNER (1987: 73)

The aim of Meisner's exercise of Breaking the Back is to replace Repetition with a playwright's text. Just as with Repetition, you say your words aloud, inflecting them with how you feel in that moment, but without consciously trying to say something meaningful. You respond to the cues you perceive in your partner's body language and tone of voice with only minimal attention to the actual words either you or they say. You are continuing to flex the muscles you have developed through Repetition of responding intuitively to your partner's non-verbal signals.

This exercise lives on only through the interpretations of former students, since there is no published account of Meisner's first-hand use of it as there is with his other key exercises. Scott Williams describes Breaking the Back as a bridging exercise between developing an actor's acting muscles and working with text. Following his own direct experiences with Meisner, he has his students sight-read a section of dialogue with no prior knowledge of the given circumstances of the text. They are asked to give minimal attention to the words they read but continue to focus their attention on their partner, allowing their partner's behaviour to affect them. In this way, meaning arises organically and often in surprising ways as the text is borne along on the currents of the actors' emotional connection, sometimes smoothly in flow together, sometimes bumping up against each other in what can be interesting and revealing eddies. Williams explains that the exercise 'allows the text to find its own true north between observing and responding'.

We do have a sense in Meisner's own words of how this exercise is useful for acting on impulses rather than cues. He explains (1987: 73) that the impulse to speak comes in response to what your partner says or does, but probably comes before the moment when it is your actual cue to speak your line. In real life we listen and think and connect and feel an impulse to say something but may have to wait our turn before we can actually say it. Meisner tells his students to 'wait for the cue, but the impulse, the emotion comes when it's felt'. Repetition is about training an actor to pick up on impulses rather than cues. Meisner adds, 'You'll get used to it once you have a command over the script. I'm saying two things to you: learn the lines; pick up the impulses.'

The key principle behind Breaking the Back is this principle of speaking on impulses rather than cues. Actor Amanda Ryan (2020) explains, 'If they look away or make a frustrated gesture whilst I am mid speech, I can take it out on my text. I can speak, fuelled by that look I just caught, over there, in the other person.' It is easy to fall into speaking a line with a preconceived sense of how we think a character means to say it, and once a pattern of how lines are spoken has been established in your mind, it is very hard to disrupt. That default position can become more and more embedded with each performance and even brings a sense of security. Mike Bernardin uses the metaphor of the spine of a book to explain the value of Breaking the Back. Patterns of reading can become apparent from how stresses on the spine cause the book to open at the pages most often read. In the same way, habitual stresses in speech can lay down patterns of practiced inflection. Breaking the Back aims to break those habits, allowing the book to open at any page so that new discoveries in speech can be made.

This exercise provides a useful gateway into speaking Shakespeare's text. As you speak your lines of Shakespeare, you will create emotional connection but the canoe of the text, as Meisner intended, is simply being buoyed along by the flow of the water as the waves and tides of emotion carry the formats and sounds of the words wherever they please. You will notice the robustness of the canoe but the limitations of Meisner's technique mean that you are not being given the skills to steer it. In the next chapter, we discuss this as a limitation of working with Meisner on Shakespeare's text.

BREAKING THE HABIT

When I teach this exercise, I say it's called 'breaking the back' because it is so painful it feels like your back is breaking, but that is more for dramatic effect. My definition is 'breaking the habit' as this tries to describe the fact that you're breaking your habitual patterns of speaking the text. It can be a very unusual experience and sometimes actors stop in a kind of shock as they realize that they have been speaking their lines in a practised inflection, or defaulting to their 'Shakespeare voice'. It is similar to hearing your own voice doing an accent wrong, or singing out of tune, and it can feel quite surprising. After doing it, everyone immediately gets it and wants to 'go again' like a scary roller coaster at a fair. The value cannot be underestimated and it is the key to a more truthful and connected rehearsal process and performance. After you've done this exercise, everyone understands how many possibilities are available to them because together you make many, many more discoveries. Butterfly actor Elle de Burgh said, 'everything in you wants to make the words make sense, have meaning and you have to resist everything and just respond and that's scary. You go giddy once you've done it because all the different possibilities tumble out.'

Exercise 3: Breaking the Back

The following adaptation of Meisner's Breaking the Back exercise offers an approach to avoid laying down patterns of delivery. It is a way into the text that takes you from uninflected line learning to beginning to find meaning in the words through your response to the other actor. This exercise is most effective if lines are learned. A good alternative, however, is for someone to feed lines, spoken neutrally, a few words at a time to the actors.

1 Create 'As Ifs' and Preparation for your character for the scene you are playing (see Chapter 7).
2 Do the imaginary work required to buy into the 'As Ifs' and Preparation, then set yourself up to do Repetition.

3   Start Repetition to test your 'As If' and Preparation.
    For example: 'You're smiling' / 'I'm smiling'; 'You're
    smiling' / 'I'm smiling'; 'You're frowning' / 'I'm frowning'
    . . . The Repetition goes back and forth between the two
    actors.

4   When your choices for 'As Ifs' and Preparation feel right, do
    steps 2 and 3 again, but this time, once Repetition has been
    established, the director calls 'text' and the actors go into
    speaking Shakespeare's lines for the scene instead of
    Repetition.

5   From now on the director has two key actions: they can call
    out 'Repetition', which means the actors go back into
    Repetition; or they can call out 'text', which means the
    actors go into speaking their lines. The director can call a
    line they want the actors to go from.

Exercise 4: *A Midsummer Night's Dream* (2.1.188–242)

Using the instructions above, try this scene between Helena and
Demetrius using the 'As Ifs' and Preparations in the two versions
below. Discuss your findings with your partner after trying both
versions. Then try another version of your own.

DEMETRIUS
  I love thee not, therefore pursue me not.
  Where is Lysander and fair Hermia?
  The one I'll stay; the other stayeth me.
  Thou toldst me they were stolen unto this wood;
  And here am I, and wood within this wood,
  Because I cannot meet my Hermia.
  Hence, get thee gone, and follow me no more.

HELENA
  You draw me, you hard-hearted adamant;
  But yet you draw not iron, for my heart
  Is true as steel. Leave you your power to draw,
  And I shall have no power to follow you.

DEMETRIUS
Do I entice you? Do I speak you fair?
Or rather do I not in plainest truth
Tell you I do not, nor I cannot love you?

HELENA
And even for that do I love you the more.
I am your spaniel, and Demetrius,
The more you beat me, I will fawn on you.
Use me but as your spaniel: spurn me, strike me,
Neglect me, loose me; only give me leave,
Unworthy as I am, to follow you.
What worser place can I beg in your love
(And yet a place of high respect with me)
Than to be used as you use your dog?

DEMETRIUS
Tempt not too much the hatred of my spirit;
For I am sick when I do look on thee.

HELENA
And I am sick when I look not on you.

Version 1: Helena and Demetrius are lost and Hermia can't be found. It's getting dark and they've just realized they're going around in circles.

Helena

- As If – someone I love desperately and want them to love me. I've overheard someone else say they do desire me.
- Preparation – sexually excited.

Demetrius

- As If – an ex who I still quite fancy and who knows something important about my new partner.
- Preparation – frustrated.

Version 2: Demetrius is lost and Hermia can't be found. Helena is following Demetrius, unaware of how lost they are. She begins the scene by jumping out from behind a tree to try yet another seductive move.

Helena

- As If – an ex who rejected me. I love them desperately and want them to love me back.
- Preparation – hopeful.

Demetrius

- As If – a one night stand I massively regret.
- Preparation – ashamed.

In Version 1 you may have found a Helena who is sexually dominant and confident and a Demetrius who is torn between his desire for her and guilt about his new partner. This might result in an interpretation of the relationship being full of conflict and power struggles, but ultimately where Helena loses.

In Version 2, you may find a Helena who is more needy and desperate and a Demetrius who feels entitled to be mean. This may suggest an interpretation of their relationship which is unequal, with Demetrius wielding power. It might come across as comic, or uncomfortable, or both.

Breaking the Back of a group scene

In a group scene, such as the wedding of Hero and Claudio in *Much Ado About Nothing*, you can try Breaking the Back, as with the two-hander scenes with free movement. If it gets too chaotic, however, limit the actors to standing in a circle. Start with everyone looking at each other and seeing a definite 'As If' for each other character in the circle. Then take a moment to get into your Preparation before you begin the scene.

Soliloquies

A soliloquy . . . needs to give the impression of being as fast as thought. It is always active and always questioning.
CICELY BERRY (2001: 175)

When working with his students on poems from Edgar Lee Masters' *The Spoon River Anthology*, Meisner (1987: 148–50) guides them to think of the texts not as poems or monologues but as speeches in a play which answer a question. He tells them to look at the last two lines of the speech to find its 'emotional essence' from which they can derive their Preparation. Used cautiously, this can be a useful exercise with Shakespeare's soliloquies. In a soliloquy, a character is thinking something through and where they end up can give clues about their emotional state coming in. For example, in *Julius Caesar* (2.1), Brutus concludes:

> And therefore think him as a serpent's egg
> Which hatched, would as his kind grow mischievous,
> And kill him in the shell.

The question he is answering is 'Why kill Caesar?' and the way his conclusion rationalizes why Caesar must die for actions not yet committed gives a strong clue about his feeling coming into the scene. Perhaps his Preparation is unease that he has not yet justified the murder to himself, or perhaps it is determination to find a reason. When Malvolio delivers Olivia's ring to Viola in *Twelfth Night* (2.2), she concludes:

> O time, thou must entangle this, not I.
> It is too hard a knot for me t'untie.

Although her Preparation coming into the scene could not include her confusion about the ring since she knows nothing about it until Malvolio arrives, her encounter with Olivia has certainly added to her sense of confusion over her whole situation and her speech is answering the question: 'Why did Olivia send this ring?' These last two lines of her soliloquy can give a strong sense of how she might feel coming into the scene – perhaps bewildered, perhaps irritated, perhaps fatalistic.

It is important to remember that a soliloquy is always a journey for a character and most importantly the actor must take the audience on the journey with them. They are keeping the audience's attention because their thoughts move the story forwards, rather than because they are simply talking about their feelings. This requires attention to the forms and structures of Shakespeare's verse, which, as we will explore further in the next chapter, is not something Meisner addresses. Where Meisner's techniques can support an actor delivering a soliloquy, however, is in emotionally engaging the audience in that journey.

The Preparation an actor brings into the scene will colour their performance, but without a fellow actor to respond to, that Preparation can only shift in response to the audience. The power of Meisner's responsive acting can be truly discovered in the direct address of soliloquies because the responsive actor will believe that *how* they are speaking is in direct response to what people in the audience are actually doing at the time (see Chapter 12). The audience then becomes part of the journey the character takes through their speech.

Summary of paraphrasing

- Paraphrasing is a process of making the writer's words have personal meaning for the actor by speaking the meaning of the words aloud in words and phrases that the actor would use in everyday speech.

- Paraphrasing is not summarizing. Actors need to be as detailed and thorough as possible in finding a version of the lines that makes most sense for them without smoothing over any difficult worlds or phrases. Glossaries in editions of the plays can be very helpful.

- The process of paraphrasing helps you to make the text your own and aligns you with the writer's intentions.

Summary of Breaking the Back

- Breaking the Back is a Meisner exercise that requires an actor to speak lines of text in response to the other actor rather than in response to what they think the lines mean.

- Lines of text are spoken aloud in the same way that the actor might speak aloud a line of Repetition, responding to impulses, not cues.

- The exercise helps the actor to discover the '93 per cent' of non-verbal communication underneath the words.

- Breaking the Back is a crucial exercise in finding freedom in speaking Shakespeare's text through finding the freedom in Meisner's methods of responding. It builds a bridge from working with Repetition to working with the writer's words.

10

The strengths and limitations of Meisner for working with Shakespeare

You've got to find out why the character needs those particular words.

JOHN BARTON (1984: 15)

Meisner has great respect for Shakespeare but it is not something he spent much time on. His respect seems at least partly based on his understanding of how Shakespeare's text viscerally affects an actor. He asks his students: 'How does one know that *Othello* is about great love and great jealousy?' and agrees when one student answers, 'You read the text and it hits you. It hits something in you' (1987: 170). Meisner demanded authentic connection raised to the optics required by the heightened nature of a dramatic text. His process is founded on an actor feeling free to express themselves fully and truthfully on stage without holding back (1987: 162), something that seems crucial to do justice to the depth and range of emotion found in Shakespeare, but his talents were not in exploring the specific riches of what it is in a Shakespeare's text that 'hits something in you'. Like many, he seems put off Shakespeare by how artificial it can sound.

Meisner (1987: 136) describes his own work as responding against a style of acting that he saw as particularly 'English'. He says acting is an 'emotional creation' for the Americans, Russians and Germans, but refers to accomplished British actors 'who know intellectually what the character should be feeling and indicate this through the way they verbally handle the text'. He is disparaging of contemporary British actors Laurence Olivier and John Gielgud, and describes a performance of Shakespeare poems by Gielgud as dependent on the beauty of his voice rather than the emotion of his delivery: 'He started off in C major; then he went to D minor. And he did each speech in a different key' (1987: 166).

This attitude can be partly put down to cultural differences. Peter Brook, who, like Meisner, has devoted his career to developing truthful acting, regards Gielgud as one of the most intuitive actors he has worked with. What appeared artificial to Meisner, the sing-songy sounds of the vocal muscularity of English actors in the early twentieth century, were developed in the different physical environment of the unforgiving acoustics of Victorian theatres, and notably the different cultural environment of British expression of emotional truth.

We can, however, still recognize Meisner's criticism of performances which rely too much on beautiful recitations of Shakespeare rather than emotionally engaging delivery. In describing 'deadly theatre', Brook (1968) finds theatre which is widely admired and respected, but which relies on tried and tested formulae rather than being alive to the moment. He suggests that Shakespeare often becomes the main casualty of deadly theatre. Audience members may enjoy a show, intellectually appreciating the ideas and performances, but feel emotionally untroubled and unaffected, or they may leave feeling excluded because even though the diction was clear, and the design was stylish, the lack of connection meant they didn't really understand what was going on. In both cases, the audience's expectations may have been met but they are not getting the full potential of what Shakespeare can offer.

The key strength of working with Meisner on Shakespeare is in raising questions about whether you are finding a genuine need to speak in response to your fellow actors in each moment of performance or whether you are just speaking beautiful poetry. The key limitation is in not appreciating how much the structures of that poetry can support you in finding your need to speak. To flourish in performing Shakespeare, you need to find the balance of Meisner's call for the full emotional commitment of actors truly in connection, matched with the technical skills of speaking the text to fill the optics of a theatre, and the specificity of thought in connecting to what you are saying and why you are saying it.

Staying truthful under Shakespeare's heightened situations

In his prologue to Longwell's account of his classes, Meisner (1987: xviii–xix) offers his favourite quote from George Bernard Shaw, 'Self-betrayal, magnified to suit the optics of the theatre, is the whole art of acting.' Meisner explains that 'self-betrayal' means 'the pure, unselfconscious revelation of the gifted actor's most inner and most private being to the people in his audience'. He expects nothing less of his students than this deep personal connection with the emotional life of a character, but he also emphasizes that their attention must be on communicating with the audience, and this means raising their performance to 'suit the optics of the theatre'. This means no mumbling or other naturalistic apologies, but truthful acting that is nevertheless big enough to fill a theatre space with the fullness of the characters' lives. His mentor Stella Adler (2000: 19) had a similar belief: 'Of course you have to bring your own experiences to bear on the characters you play, but you have to realise right from the outset that Hamlet was not "a guy like you".'

The heightened nature of Shakespeare's text and the lives of his characters can sometimes feel too big to be able to fill adequately. Meisner stresses the importance of making emotion fuller, by which he means deeper, not bigger, as the way to find the emotional depth needed to inhabit characters beyond our everyday understanding. His key to unlocking how to make your performance deeper is to raise the stakes and choose things that *really* matter to you. Find an 'As If' that is extreme but still just within the bounds of reality, daydreams of real shame, real joy, real sorrow that truly affects you. Remember, however that acting is primarily a job, not therapy. Meisner was very clear that memories, whether joyous or traumatic, are often less powerful, and certainly less easy to control, than your imagination. Use your imagination to build personal stories that take you out of your comfort zone, but don't push against your mental health. You don't need to pick the recent death of your father or your marriage break-up to connect to real hurt, betrayal or sorrow.

If you are playing Hermia, for example, in *A Midsummer Night's Dream*, how can you connect to the terrible choice she faces at the start of the play if she refuses to marry Demetrius (1.1.65–78)? What if you imagine the situation 'As If' you will be locked away in solitary confinement or 'As If' you live in a country where honour killings are sanctioned. Most of us are fortunate that our own fears can lead us to imagine situations far worse than the reality of our lived experiences. Despotic kings and tyrants in the plays can be related to by imagining more power given to leaders that you consider malicious or dangerously irrational. Imagine that leader now has the power to order the death penalty at will. You may also want to consider social death. Avoiding shame is a very strong human drive. How would you feel if naked photos or sex videos of you were posted on social media? How would you feel if you'd written a long email complaining about your boss to your friend, and you accidentally press 'send all' so that your boss gets the email too? Imagine anything that makes you feel sick to your stomach and makes your heart race. The idea of your parents seeing those pictures or your boss reading what you wrote about them can make you fight for something in order to prevent it. Whatever you imagine to take yourself into the right emotional territory, it is important to take yourself out of it too. Working on an extract from *Spring Awakening* by Frank Wedekind, Meisner (1987: 200) pushes two of his actors to find a depth of emotion that makes them sob uncontrollably. When the scene is done, he tells them to sing, to laugh, to tickle themselves – anything in order to move them out of that dark emotional place back into the light.

Meisner's techniques offer highly practical ways into finding your personal connections to the given circumstances of the text and allowing you to live truthfully from the point of view of a character. They support you in raising your performance to meet the optics of the theatre, finding a depth in your performance to play the size and intensity of Shakespeare's characters. Equally important in working with Shakespeare, however, is to allow the language itself to affect you.

Staying truthful under Shakespeare's heightened text

Rehearsing the scene mentioned above from *Spring Awakening*, Meisner (1987: 195–201) pushes the two women to cry and cry hard from the beginning of the scene. He pushes them to improvise the words they need in the moment, not reach for their lines, and he tells them to be in this highly emotionally charged state from the start of the scene, not to work up to it or look for any sort of journey. He reminds them of his key metaphor that text is the canoe on a river of emotion, and tells them they are both in a fragile canoe together on a tempestuous river. They produce a performance that Longwell (1987: 200) describes as 'full of tears and emotionally moving, but the amount of their emotion and inexperience in handling it makes it difficult for the audience to understand every word'. Meisner (1987: 200) is unconcerned about this. He explains that his 'chief concern' is for his actors 'to act out the life of the scene as intended by the playwright' and that once they have invested in that emotional life, 'the clarity will come by itself. The canoe won't capsize.'

Meisner trusts that a playwright's words spoken by an actor deeply in connection with the given circumstances of the text will take care of themselves. Many directors prefer not to analyse the technicalities of Shakespeare's text too closely and instead focus on how it sounds to the modern ear. This can create highly engaging productions, but not exploring the possibilities of how the text works can also limit the potential of how an actor can use that text. With Shakespeare, you are not speaking just a playwright's words, you are speaking some of the most powerful poetic language we have in our social treasury. Cicely Berry (2001: 3), former Director of Voice and Text for the Royal Shakespeare Company, tells us Shakespeare's writing 'is much more extreme' than modern naturalistic dramas, 'and the modern actor must connect with the extravagance of the image yet make it sound as if spoken for now'. John Barton (1984: 135), one of the founding directors of the RSC, warns of 'the naturalistic fallacy that emotion communicates better than words'. He and Berry were not interested in actors merely speaking beautiful poetry; instead they wanted to explore how Shakespeare's forms and structures can work on the subconscious of an actor to clarify and drive their character's intentions. Berry describes this personal connection as 'the meeting between the intention of the character and the imagination of the actor which is then released into the word'. Barton (1984: 117) warns that an actor 'must never become bound or bogged down' by detailed text work but that if they can understand and absorb how Shakespeare uses and plays with rhythms, alliterations, antithesis, metaphors, rhymes and other literary devices, 'if he can find his way through it and make friends with the text, he will become not bound, but more free'.

Once actors get past their fears and 'make friends with the text', they can find huge freedom in working with the nuances and ambiguities in the language and the human inconsistencies in the characters. Because Shakespeare provides the words we rarely find in our own lives to express how we feel, inhabiting his characters and speaking his words can feel immensely energizing for an actor and deeply satisfying for an audience to hear. As Berry (1987: 39) explains, 'there is a pleasure at being that articulate, but the pleasure is not to do with being elaborate and poetic, it is to do with release of feeling, and the ability to be explicit about it'. Barton and Berry both called for a 'balancing act' that pays attention to the technical details of the text and honours the structures of Shakespeare's writing, while still sounding truthful to the modern ear. As actor Amanda Ryan (2020) describes,

> With Shakespeare, I've always thought firstly about the text. I put work into where do I breathe, where's the break, what's the rhythm, what's the important word in this line. Has the line got more or less beats? There's a lot of studying I like to do outside of any interaction. So that I know what it is that I'm communicating. Then I feel I can read and respond with all of that in place.

Canoeing with Shakespeare

The practices of Meisner, Barton and Berry all aim to support an actor in finding truth in the moment. There is, however, a very clear contradiction, not just in their starting points, but also in their focus on where truth comes from. For Berry, 'words are thoughts in action'. Her belief is that we should start with the words to engage with the thoughts of the character because thoughts give rise to feelings, not the other way round. She says, 'It is how we *think* that is interesting, and not how we *feel*' (2001: 138, italics original) because 'if the thought does not come through with clarity we lose the reason for the feeling and this leads to generalization, a wash of sentimentality' (2001: 20). Meisner, on the other hand, had a sign clearly displayed in his classroom that read 'Act Before You Think', asserting his focus (explored throughout this book) on feeling before thinking.

Meisner's techniques are about developing and deepening an actor's connection to the river of their emotions, as described in his famous metaphor of the text as a canoe:

> The text is like a canoe ... and the river in which it sits is the emotion. The text floats on the river. If the water of the river is turbulent, the words will come out like a canoe on a rough river. It all depends on the flow of the river which is your emotion. The text takes on the character of your emotion.
>
> 1987: 115

Once he can see that the river is flowing freely, he asks his actors to take more control of the canoe, to find a reason for every moment (1987: 235) and to 'Know why you say everything you say' (1987: 224), but his primary emphasis remains on the river. For understanding of the canoe and how it works with the river to shape a journey, the Shakespearean actor needs to look elsewhere.

When Berry (1987: 61) worked with North American actors in New York, she was excited about 'the bringing together of the UK tradition bedded in the spoken word, with the "Method" work of US actors and its focus on the inner emotional drive'. She worked with actors trained by Group Theatre alumni, during a project in New York with Theatre for a New Audience, and found how symbiotically her techniques with text could work with those actors' more psychologically focused training. She saw this in essence as the reconciling of argument versus emotion, finding that her ways of inhabiting the language worked in parallel with their ways of inhabiting the character. Her practice allowed them to clarify the thoughts in the text, releasing the reasoning which goes hand in hand with the emotion so they could inhabit the moment with the character's full weight of both thought and feeling. She explains, 'It made the words the discovering element, for if you fill the words only with the feeling of the character, there is no discovery left' (2001: 63).

Research has shown how our emotions are essential to any thoughts we have and how thoughts sort and shape emotions into concepts we can express to others through verbal language. Our ideas are fed by feelings and those feelings are clarified through words. Berry describes how language originated 'as noises expressing a need, a feeling, an intent, whether of anger or frustration or desire, to another human being' (2001: 3), and her work was designed to bring about a visceral understanding of thoughts and emotions interwoven. Meisner's techniques are often regarded as anti-intellectual, focusing on impulses and instinctive responses, but this need not preclude a sensitivity to the words a playwright gives. The Shakespearean actor needs both mind and body working at full capacity in order to be fully responsive to the thoughts and feelings that arise in their given circumstances in each and every moment of their performance. Meisner seems to understand this himself when he praises his student Joseph for his progress in becoming more relaxed at engaging emotionally in a scene, but suggests he now needs to work harder on sharpening the details and finding a reason for each moment of the script. He tells Joseph, 'Emotionally freer, yet you still don't know why you say what you say at each moment. You should have both' (1987: 235).

Asked about the most important thing when playing Shakespeare, Peggy Ashcroft said, 'the truth', adding, 'What do we mean by truth? Truth of reality. Truth of poetry, which is a little bit of super-reality. And truth of character. It's the fusion of poetry, truth and character that is required in Shakespeare' (Barton, 1984: 207–8). A Shakespearean actor can work symbiotically with the canoe of text that Meisner describes to play the truth which is always at the heart of his work – not by jumping in and being carried wherever the current of emotions lead, but by learning the skills to steer a sleek, efficient canoe crafted by Shakespeare, designed to respond with utmost sensitivity to the waters it journeys with.

Summary of strengths

- The heightened size of the text and characters is filled by the actors' own deep truthful connections and river of emotions.
- The emotions of the audience are more truthfully engaged when the actors themselves make a truthful connection with Shakespeare's text.

Summary of limitations

- If the text is reduced only to a canoe being buffeted by emotions, there is a lack of specificity.
- The power of the words themselves does not get unleashed.

PART THREE

Aileen Gonsalves in conversation with Tracy Irish about how Butterfly Theatre Company use Meisner's techniques

11

Taking Meisner's principles into the practice of Butterfly Theatre Company's 'Five Conditions'

The first thing you have to do with a text is find yourself.
SANFORD MEISNER (1987: 178)

Who are Butterfly Theatre Company?

Butterfly are a collection of around fifty actors, directors and writers. Most of us have been working together now for more than ten years. When I set up this company, I knew I needed a group of actors who had a shared language and ethos and who not only trusted me but each other. Our like-minded group began to form around the Meisner principles but the Meisner purists kept saying, 'But it's not Meisner!' We agreed our work is *rooted in* Meisner and I always referred to it as 'Aileen's Meisner', or 'The Gonsalves Method' as I call it now. My method basically describes 'Five Conditions' (see below) for creating any character in relationship with another and was my way of creating workable, affectable given circumstances under which actors could live truthfully.

We wanted to create site-specific, immersive productions, mainly Shakespeare, in extraordinary places such as cave labyrinths, historic castles and ancient woodlands in the UK and Europe – and so Butterfly Theatre Company was born. It became the resident theatre company attached to the MA in Acting at ArtsEd Drama School where I was the Head of the course. Because we were so interested in cause and effect, the name Butterfly came from 'the butterfly effect' – an illustration of chaos theory that a butterfly flapping its wings in one place or time can result in a tornado in another. Our company is built on the principle of 'discovery first'. We use whatever is at our disposal, trustingly putting our performance into each other's hands so that, using Meisner's metaphor, we can truly say ouch when we are pinched! Non-theatre spaces allow us to keep focused on truthful connection with our audiences. You cannot lie when they are a metre away from you in shared light – and sometimes shared dark if your breath accidentally blows out the only candle, plunging everyone into darkness!

Why has Meisner been so influential on your practice?

Our bedrock is Meisner's exercise of Repetition – through which my company have all found freedom and which we love. It is the only thing I have ever seen or worked with that consistently allows actors to stay out of their heads and fully connect to the other actor. From the first time I saw it to now, I always notice how people are so amazed and relieved to be truthfully connecting with someone. It's truly liberating. My directing and teaching career has centred on finding ways to maintain that freedom under the given circumstances of any text, under any direction, in front of any audience night after night. I wanted to keep the actor as free as they feel with Repetition but still adhering to the writer's intention, the director's direction and the unpredictability of other actors and the audience. We began to experiment as a company. Because we were working on a fantastically reliable constant – Shakespeare – we could really test and risk and test again. Through a lot of trial and error our Five Conditions became more and more refined, tested in the safety of the rehearsal room and under the demands of live performance.

What limitations have you found in working with Meisner techniques on Shakespeare?

The challenge with Meisner and Shakespeare is Meisner's metaphor about 'text as the canoe on a river of emotion'. How can that be true of Shakespeare's extraordinary text? Early on in our experiments using Meisner techniques, we found that the plays worked really well on a visceral level and had an aliveness and vividness that felt satisfying, but ultimately we knew we were missing specificity of expression and that moments were disappearing because we were losing the power of the words. When I worked with Cicely Berry and explored her work, exploring the 'need to speak', the circle was completed for me. The other constant challenge with Shakespeare is the almost perverse way we learn lines with no inflection and absolutely no meaning. Shakespeare's rhythm and what we absorb as the right or 'appropriate' way of speaking it (learnt from watching productions or how we were taught) is always screaming in your head. This led to extreme ways of tackling uninflected line learning; however, we recognized we couldn't ignore the basis of iambic pentameter in Shakespeare's writing – once we started rehearsing with the text, we found the rhythm was in everyone's bones (see chapter 8). I am so bold as to say that learning lines uninflected, and 'beyond learning' as we say, is the only way to make Meisner work effectively with Shakespeare, if not with any text, but it needs to be done with an awareness and sensitivity to how the metre works.

How have you adapted Meisner's key exercises and concepts for how you work with Shakespeare?

The Reality of Doing: In working with the concept of the Reality of Doing, I focus on how being observed when you are carrying out an activity, such as counting the blinds or the floorboards, can cause you to go back into your head and unhelpfully judge how others see you. It is no great sin to go back in your head – in fact it is impossible to stay out of it all the time – but it is useful to identify the two different states. You are then more aware of the need to come back out of your head every time you go back in.

Repetition: When working with any actors, the Listing exercise (see Chapter 3) is my key for giving you a consistent way of coming out of your head and unlocking working on text using Meisner. Through this exercise, you realize experientially that you are not seeing as clearly as you thought, or at least you realize there is always more to see. This exercise then becomes a great introduction into Repetition. We follow the Listing by ensuring everyone is giving themselves permission to 'fuck polite' and be honest in their responses, which the Building Permission exercise creates (see Chapter 3).

The exercises I developed for using Repetition in chapter 4 are purposefully created to lead to working on text. For me it is important with Repetition to 'speak with how you feel and do what your partner makes you want to do'. This helps when the text comes into play in using the words to get your objective, as it affects your tone of voice (see next chapter for more on this). It also helps when staging as you can form physical habits of being bold in your responses in Repetition, which again push you to make bolder choices in the moment of rehearsal and performance. Unusually I constantly interject during Repetition, exhorting people to 'Speak with how you feel', 'Do what they make you want to do' and 'Let it matter'. I do this to encourage permission as a stepping stone to working with our 'Five Conditions'; then my main call as director is: 'Is it working?'

Given Circumstances: You can use all the information and analysis found in your knowledge lists (see Chapter 6) to create your character's *point of view*. This means seeing clearly and responding honestly, not from *your* point of view, but your character's. The 'Five Conditions' are a way of corralling all the knowledge from the lists into five simple conditions which you work out, consider and do off stage. It's very much 'in your head work' done in the wings, which colours what you do on stage in the moment, allowing you to be out of your head and able to respond to the other actor. The Five Conditions can change what you see, and if you change what you see, you can change how you respond.

The other exercises of Independent Activity and Knock on the Door and the concepts of Preparation and As Ifs are woven into how we use the Five Conditions.

Can you explain what the Five Conditions are and how they work?

The Five Conditions are created from the knowledge lists (see Chapter 6) and become our workable given circumstances. Butterfly actor Carla-Marie Metcalfe explains, 'Gathering all the facts and finding everything that's at your disposal to use is very exciting. From then on ideas just pop into your head all the time – you start making loads of little connections.' We rehearse using Repetition to find how we can 'live truthfully' under these conditions. All the Five Conditions have to be done off stage or in the wings, and they have to be tested with full commitment. They have to be able to be tested using Repetition only, so they cannot be too wordy – the simpler the better. They have to affect your own heart as you construct them and they need to trigger you emotionally when you imagine them. I realized making the audience feel something real only happens if the actor feels something real, and that only happens if your attention is out and on the other actor, so the Conditions have to be all about the other person. It came down to simply considering:

1 How am I feeling before seeing them? – **Prep**
2 Who is the person I am talking to in my imagination? – **As If**
3 What am I trying to get them to do? – **Objective**
4 Why do they have to do it now? – **Stakes**
5 Why do I deserve for them to give me my Objective?
   – **Entitlement**

Prep: Essentially this is Meisner's Preparation but we also adapted the Knock on the Door exercise into the 'Prep' condition by taking away the need for a door. We were working in caves and forests and had lots of quick changes, so we needed a quick way into each new scene. Meisner's Preparation gives us how we come into the scene, and the first moment of eye contact between actors is the equivalent of the Knock on the Door.

There are many ways to get into Preps, so you need to find the most effective ways that work for you as a trigger. You need something that makes you deeply feel an emotion off stage to change your state for the first moment of the scene. You use your imagination to tap into the right daydream. In Butterfly we also use the eight physical Laban efforts because they are so immediate and effective. Rudolf Laban was a Hungarian movement practitioner who developed a system of describing movement in terms of weight, space and time. This results in eight 'efforts' that can affect us deeply as they come from the body, but can also be shaken off quickly. A useful book to find out more is *Laban's Efforts in Action: A Movement Handbook for Actors with Online Video Resources* by Vanessa Ewan and Kate Sagovsky. Using Laban, Butterfly actors 'prep up' in a corner of the rehearsal room. They jump about 'punching' or 'dab' around with excitement, or 'wring' with some angst – we never ask what anyone is thinking, that is always private. When each actor is ready they come into the space. If it takes longer for one actor to arrive, the other one waits in the Prep state, using the waiting to feed whatever Prep they have. For example, if your Prep is 'nervous', you let the fact that they are not ready yet unnerve you. Or if 'excited' you let the waiting for them feed your anticipation and excitement. When both actors are ready and make eye contact, that moment begins the exercise. They shift their attention from themselves to the other and allow themselves to be totally affectable.

As If: The 'As If' condition is again essentially taken from Meisner's concept of particularization or 'as ifs'. In Butterfly we tend to focus on the substitution element with the 'As If'. Using your imagination you simply change how you see the other actor (see 'As If' descriptions in Chapter 7). It is incredibly useful, fast and effective. It is good for a director to use as it helps actors make changes and play very efficiently. The audience cannot read your mind but they feel what you feel – that is the great power of the actor. So as an audience we project the feeling we get from the actor on to the story and characters we are watching, and the connection is complete. Butterfly actor Charis King says, 'The As If instantly changes everything.' We ensure we have an imaginary connection, an 'As If' on all people, places and things that we or our acting partner talk about. These 'As If' connections become essential when we start using the text to get our Objectives.

Objectives, Stakes and Entitlement: These conditions formed the breakthrough in our understanding of how to use Meisner with Shakespeare, or indeed any text. We started to experiment with the idea of the Independent Activity – where an actor sets up a task that is difficult but achievable, and which aims for an outcome that is important to them. We made the task that needs to be completed in the Independent Activity into the character's Objective. The reason for completing the task then became the character's Stakes. Another thing we explored was how to talk about objectives. The usual way of describing objectives as 'I want ...' is not directly about completing a task, so we just turn around the wording so that 'I want ...' becomes 'Get them to ...'. The Objective is then rooted in the other person and can only be achieved by having your attention fully on that other person. In this way your performance becomes dependent on the other actor.

This allows the actor and director to continually ask, 'Is it working?' Can you see from the other person's behaviour and hear from what they are saying that you are achieving your Objective? What are the body language, tone and other physical 'cues' telling you about whether it's working or not? You will discover either it is going well, in which case you keep building on whatever tactics you are currently using, or if it looks like you are failing to achieve your Objective, then you know you have to change tactics and try something else.

Adding Stakes to your Objectives is essential as Stakes are what matters to your character, the fire in their belly driving them to achieve their Objective. We describe the Stakes as both positive and negative, because you can be driven by either hope of success or fear of failure. We added Entitlement as a way of strengthening the impact of Objectives and Stakes. 'They *should* give it to me. I deserve it.' This sense of entitlement, like 'As Ifs', and Stakes should be something *you* can personally relate to; it need not be directly connected to the play (see below for examples).

Working with Preparations and As Ifs has been discussed earlier in this book (in Chapter 7), but can you say more about Objectives, Stakes and Entitlement and how you create those conditions?

It's worth considering how we play objectives in everyday life. A teenager trying to get money from an adult is a great example. Most teenagers intuitively know how to read their parents' moods according to behavioural clues. They then try tactics from a well-used palette that they know has previously achieved success, such as flattery, bartering or making puppy dog eyes. If a tactic is 'working', they build on it relentlessly until they get the money; if not, they reach for another tactic to try. Characters in Shakespeare's plays are doing the same. In Act 1, Scene 7 of *Macbeth*, for example, we understand that overall Lady Macbeth's Objective on Macbeth is to 'Get him to kill Duncan', but in our process that is the Stakes rather than the Objective. The actor needs to choose something more concrete that can be achieved and observed in the rehearsal room, such as 'Get him to agree with me' or 'Get him to be strong'. Because if he does that, he will then kill Duncan. Make the Objective something very tangible so that you can see clearly whether it's working or not in their behaviour. In order for this to be tangible, it needs to be something that matters to you personally and that you can imagine. Killing a king will not be in your personal realm of experience, so you need to find something equivalent, which could be imagining killing a family member to profit from their will.

A way to summarize the conditions of Objective, Stakes and Entitlement for the teenager in a sentence could be: 'Get them to trust me because if they trust me they'll give me the money but if they don't trust me they won't give me the money and they should trust me because I'm always home when I say I will be home.' This **Golden Sentence** construction can be applied to any scene to check your Objectives, Stakes and Entitlement are in the right territory. With Lady Macbeth, the sentence might be: 'Get him to be strong because if he is strong he will kill a family member so I can be all powerful and if he isn't strong he won't kill the family member and I will become insignificant and he should be strong because I'm his wife and I'm always right and he loves me!'

It's good to have one Objective per scene. A scene in this case is when a character enters the stage to when they leave the stage. Challenge yourself to find an all-encompassing Objective that captures what is going on across the entirety of a scene. If an 'unexpected event' then happens, like a letter arriving, you just need to ask whether the thing that has occurred is good or bad for your Objective. While rehearsing, try to keep Objectives a secret from the other actors playing the scenes – it's much more fun!

If you add in As Ifs and Preps, you can see how the Five Conditions work together. In the Lady Macbeth example above, think about what can happen if you add that you see Macbeth 'As If' he's a stubborn ex-boyfriend that you know still fancies you, adding that your Prep is 'frustrated'. We keep each Condition as simple as possible. The complexity comes with the cumulative mix of Conditions brought to life through the unique actors in response to each other moment by moment as they deal with my shouted call, 'Is it working?' The actors' personal connections with the Conditions will produce internal pulls, tears and inner obstacles. For this reason, it is important to ensure that actors do not change the Conditions by themselves as it is the *combination* that makes the scene what it is. Butterfly director Jen McGregor explains how actors using this technique are 'incredibly affectable and can cope with anything you throw at them'. She adds, 'I love changing a Condition and within three seconds we all know it's wrong and even tend to know why and how to adjust it.'

Can you give another example of how the Five Conditions would work with a Shakespeare scene?

Example: *Romeo and Juliet* (2.2.49–193)

If you are directing the balcony scene in *Romeo and Juliet*, you need to consider how *you* want to frame this very famous scene. Are you looking for a stronger or weaker Juliet, a more knowing one or a more innocent one, a more practical or more petulant? A more lustful Romeo or romantic, unsure or headstrong? To start with, you need to root your choices in the text by using the Knowledge Lists (see Chapter 6) for both Romeo and Juliet – which the actors should create for themselves. On the basis of this information, directors decide Five Conditions in discussion with each actor and try them out. Consider these two versions and ask yourself:

- What kind of relationship might you get with these Conditions?
- Where might the power lie?

- Where might the audience sympathies lie?
- What kind of character might emerge with these Conditions?
- How much permission do they have?

Version 1

Romeo
As If – A woman I desire who I know desires me.
Prep – excited.
Objective – get them to make the first move.
Positive Stakes – because if they make the first move they will agree to be mine.
Negative Stakes – because if they don't make the first move I may never see them again and I'll have lost the love of my life.
Entitlement – they kissed me on the dance floor. I am the most eligible guy in town and I just overheard them saying how much they like me!

Juliet
As If – gorgeous guy who was an amazing kisser but who I've heard is a player about town.
Prep – frustrated.
Objective – get them to take me seriously.
Positive Stakes – because if they take me seriously they will not get caught and they'll agree to marry me.
Negative Stakes – because if they don't take me seriously, they'll get caught and I may never see them again and I'll have lost the love of my life.
Entitlement – I kissed them on the dance floor. I am the most eligible girl in town.

Good luck Romeo! That's going to be quite hard work for him in this combination of Conditions, as Juliet needs to be won over. In this version, you could see a Romeo who appears cocky, impetuous and energized and a Juliet who is torn between desire and practicalities. This may give an interpretation that their relationship is youthful, impetuous and built more on lust.

Version 2

In this version we are adding the environmental circumstances of the presence on the Capulet estate of guard dogs. Romeo has overheard Juliet speaking secretly about her feelings towards him, but he didn't catch everything she said because he was watching out for dogs. She knows that a guard dog savaged an intruder last week.

Romeo

As If – a beautiful woman who is way out of my league.

Prep – nervous.

Objective – get them to commit fully to me.

Positive Stakes – because if they commit fully to me we can be together.

Negative Stakes – because if they don't commit fully to me, I may never see them again and I'll have lost the love of my life.

Entitlement – they kissed me on the dance floor. I am the most eligible guy in town.

Juliet

As If – a gorgeous guy who I've fancied for ages but never told.

Prep – excited.

Objective – get them to take me seriously.

Positive Stakes – because if they take me seriously they will leave now and not get caught and I can hope to see them again.

Negative Stakes – because if they don't take me seriously they'll get caught and hurt and I'll have lost the love of my life.

Entitlement – I really love them. I'm really smart. I'm the most eligible girl in town.

In this version you might see a Romeo who is less sure of himself and wants to be respectful and careful, and a Juliet who appears very practical and is torn between her feelings and her situation. This may give an interpretation that their relationship is more innocent and earnest.

Summary of Butterfly's Five Conditions

The Five Conditions, developed by Butterfly Theatre Company, form a rehearsal process rooted in Meisner's techniques. In combination, they create a character's point of view and colour how the actor sees things through that character's eyes. The Five Conditions are: As If, Prep, Objective, Stakes and Entitlement. Butterfly use mainly substitutions for 'As Ifs' to change whom you are talking to or about. They use Preps as triggers to get into the right emotional place. They describe Objectives as: 'Get them to . . .'. This construction allows them to check: 'Is it working?' Tactics in attempting to achieve the Objective are found in the moment in response to a fellow actor. If your tactic is working, you keep going; if it's failing, you change. With Stakes, it is important to imagine something that matters to *you*, not just the character. You need a sense of Entitlement in order to understand why you deserve to achieve your Objective. Their Golden Sentence is: Get them to [Objective] because if they do I'll get [Positive Stakes] and if they don't [Objective] I won't get [Negative Stakes] and they should [Objective] because [Entitlement].

12

Taking Meisner's principles into the practice of Butterfly Theatre Company's work with Shakespeare's text

It's an exhilarating, scary feeling looking at each other knowing we don't know exactly what is going to happen – then going out there knowing you're completely safe, the Conditions are done, the cast is all with you – then just seeing the amazement on the audience's faces as they run along with you, painting this canvas together, making it happen together.

BUTTERFLY ACTOR OLIVER TOWSE

As discussed in previous chapters, Meisner's expertise was not in working with Shakespeare. As a theatre company who mainly work with Shakespeare, how has Meisner helped you with text work?

Line Learning: We believe that uninflected line learning is the key to making Shakespeare authentic and alive and we are unrelenting and rigorous about it. When running lines, if we hear each other inflect, even for a second, we jump on them (sometimes literally). Butterfly actor Caroline Colomei explains, 'Knowing them so well so your lines can just fly off your tongue, it's such a gift, it's magic, it's freedom.' We want the words deep in our long-term memories so that we can remain 'unthinking' in our responses when performing. How you *learn* the lines directly affects how you perform them. A good tip, for instance, is to keep your attention fixed on something as you run lines on your own – this trains you to keep your attention outwards yet not lose the lines. We are always very physical while running lines, and play lots of games. The games mean you have to be able to say the lines while being focused outward on whatever might happen in the game. The idea is that anything can happen and you can still say the lines. 'Beyond learning' is a term we developed because there is a breakthrough moment when you no longer have to think, the words just come out. As Butterfly actor Matthew McPherson describes, 'If you don't learn lines ahead of rehearsals then you're just line learning and dressing it up as rehearsing.'

When we are rehearsing, we find knowing the lines so completely makes the Breaking the Back exercise really valuable. It allows Shakespeare's words to be as free as the phrases we use in Repetition. However, the danger of learning in an uninflected way is that you only learn the lines in a monotone way and it becomes a pattern in itself. So we speak the lines going up and down the scale when learning, as that breaks up the pattern. It also frees the voice and allows you to habitually use your full range – which becomes really useful for finding full vocal expression in the 'chair exercise' (see below) when using the words to get your objective. Doing all these odd things when learning the lines means that, by default, more freedom is available to you when performing. Because how you learn lines ends up being how you say them, you also need to be alert to how fast you are running them and be wary of gabbling. Sometimes we do a diction line run to help our mouths get around the words while learning. We run lines before every rehearsal, and before every performance if we can, and if there is a problem when rehearsing a scene or we get stuck, we always just do a quick line run to check whether the problem is happening because the actors are still in their heads holding onto control because they still don't fully know the lines. Butterfly director Nicholas Humphries adds, 'By agreeing to give up control the actors gain a lot of control because they become empowered to adapt what is there and make it work for them.'

Paraphrasing: Paraphrasing with Shakespeare is a common enough exercise, but I realized that we were not being specific enough. So we have broken up paraphrasing into stages. We recognize that we need to look up what every word and reference means by looking at notes and glossaries, but we also understand that knowing what something means is not the same as how *we* would say it. When we paraphrase, we always put the text into language we would use in our own lives. That distinction really helps us own the language much more and naturally leads us to consider the best 'As If' connections. Butterfly actor Hayley Cusick says, 'I find a lot of those Ohs and Ays become common phrases that I use on the daily, like "Oh for goodness' sake" and suddenly the text becomes a lot less scary and a lot more familiar and I'm not spending three hours trying to work out how I might say "Ay me".' We go slowly with our texts and notes to hand so we can really be specific about everything and everyone we talk about or hear about. This ensures we inhabit the discoveries we made in our knowledge lists so that they can actually affect us in the moment. It is a very 'in our heads' stage but means we can be free for the next stage. It also makes us realize how much of Shakespeare's text is how we would say it normally, which can reassure and inspire actors in the company who may be fearing it is a completely foreign language.

Breaking the Back: The aim of Breaking the Back for Meisner was to replace Repetition with a playwright's text, continuing his foundational concept that you speak your lines in response to the other actor rather than in response to what you think your lines mean. You respond intuitively to your partner's non-verbal signals, their tone of voice as well as the words you hear them say. We added to this that you are also speaking under the Five Conditions. These Conditions colour *how* you respond to your partner, whether you are speaking Repetition or Shakespeare's text. Adding the Five Conditions to Breaking the Back really gave us the bridge into working with Shakespeare and getting away from what we call the 'Shakespeare voice', which is when people put on the accent they think Shakespeare should be spoken in. Saying Shakespeare's text while doing Breaking the Back can feel like the most perverse exercise because you have to fight against making sense of the words, but it really helps (see Chapter 11). It pushes you into a more truthful connection with the text as you are too busy checking if you're getting your Objective to be poetic. Butterfly actor Sophie Rickman describes it quite poetically, saying, 'It's like lighting a candle; the language is the wax, and the wick and the structure and the flame is the unique person responding in the moment.' This exercise exposes actors going back inside their heads as they immediately sound false when they do – and it can also highlight when lines are not learned fully. If either of these things happen, it's very important to laugh about it and reassure your actors it happens to everyone – they've just gone in their heads and need to get their attention outwards.

Who else has influenced your work with Shakespeare's text and how has this manifested in your practice?

My English teacher at secondary school, Catherine Lillington, engendered the great love I have for Shakespeare, as her passion was infectious and she made it feel connected and something that I could use to express myself. It is the greatest joy that she comes to see Butterfly productions whenever she can. Bizarrely, over the years watching untruthful, painful, laboured, 'deadly' Shakespeare has been a very big inspiration and is always a 'spur to prick the sides of my intent'. But thankfully working with Cicely Berry was the key that unlocked the text for me. The way she talked about the power of the words and how she managed to release that in actors with her various exercises to discover their real need to speak completely inspired me. Meisner's Repetition coupled with the Five Conditions and Cicely's work allowed me to develop exercises that gave specificity and released the power of the words without upending the 'canoe'. This combination allowed us to effortlessly but skilfully navigate moment to moment and use the words to get our objectives. I have sat alongside Gregory Doran, Artistic Director at the RSC, as an assistant and associate director, and he holds a meticulous first fortnight of rehearsals with the whole company unpicking possibilities for what the text means. I saw how this got everybody on the same page and this influenced how I adapted my paraphrasing stages. I saw Mark Rylance as Hamlet really ask the audience, 'Am I a coward?' and I saw hundreds of people including myself panic because we felt he wanted us to answer him there and then, and we really had to consider the question. In that moment I understood what truthful connection could be like in a Shakespeare play. He and Shakespeare had made me feel something real. And it goes without saying, but of course the years of discussions about text I've had with my co-author!

Can you share some of the additional exercises you use in Butterfly for working with Shakespeare's text?

Exercise 1: Back to Back

In Chapter 4, we outlined Meisner's repetition game. One of his adaptations of the exercise included the actors not looking at each other. This seemed to me extremely useful for getting actors to really listen and be affected by their partner and, now the words are in use, for actors to hear how well or badly they are doing at getting their Objective. The small sighs, laughs, in-breaths and tone of voice they hear from their partner are all things to tune into, and any silences can be particularly telling. Back to Back simply means standing with your back to your partner and speaking your text. Doing the exercise **without touching** is very important, as we get a huge amount of physical impulses once we touch. The silence at the start of this exercise is a particularly powerful way into the first moment. We do the exercise in two stages:

Stage 1: Back to Back with Repetition and the Five Conditions

* Do Repetition back to back with your Five Conditions in place and notice how they affect what happens. For example: 'You're shuffling' / 'I'm shuffling'; 'You're breathing' / 'I'm breathing'; 'You're laughing' / 'I'm laughing' . . .

- Consider an 'As If' that your boss is behind you. If they are not talking or they sound grumpy or flirtatious, how will that affect how you respond, compared to an 'As If' on your partner as a junior colleague?
- Do your Prep fully beforehand without any physical restrictions. Jump about or run around or whatever is needed, and then stand in your position.
- It can be tricky to try to get your Objectives when you are back to back, but once the text is introduced in the next stage, you will hear if it is working or not by how your partner is speaking or not speaking, and by what they are saying.
- Consider your Stakes before you do any version of the scene, as these keep you on track and help you let things matter. The same can be said of Entitlement.

Stage 2: Back to Back with text and the Five Conditions

Now try the Back to Back exercise, exactly as above, except for replacing Repetition with the lines of the text. You are now speaking in response to what you hear, or don't hear, behind you. You now can truly hear if it is working by the *words* they are saying. For example, if your Objective is to get someone to kiss you and you hear them say the text, 'You've got soft lips', it's very different from hearing them say, 'You've got bad breath.' Always consider whether what is being said to you is good or bad for your Objective. When Romeo hears Juliet say, 'If they do see thee, they will murder thee' (2.2.70), it is entirely different from later in the scene when she says, 'My bounty is as boundless as the sea' (2.2.133).

Most important in this exercise is that you do not try to give meaning to your *own* words; instead you are tuned into *your partner's* words. This focus outwards to your partner allows you to be surprised by the words you yourself speak and the meaning you find through them, which keeps them fresh each time you speak them.

This Back to Back exercise brings together Meisner's emphasis on response and Berry's emphasis on language to explore how text can fully come to life when you have made a particular connection to everything you speak. What you hear will now have a real emotional impact by default of you and your scene partners having found 'As Ifs' for all the people, places and things you talk about or hear about, and having paraphrased Shakespeare's text into your own words with the resonances of those 'As Ifs'. Once you have really heard the words, your need to speak gets intensified.

Exercise 2: Using your words to get your Objective

What if, as Cicely Berry asked, 'Your only weapon is your words'? All the elements of Shakespeare's use of language – the rhetorical and poetic devices, the use of vowels and consonants, antithesis, alliteration, onomatopoeia, assonance, rhyme, rhythm, etc. – become the literary precision weapons in your arsenal of ways to build on any tactic that you can see is working, or if you're failing they can help you change tactic. The exercise outlined below is developed from Berry's Displacement Activities and is the one I have found most useful in the rehearsal process. It is rooted in Berry's exercises on resistance where an actor speaks their lines and tries to reach another actor while being physically held back or trying to break through a barrier of people. For Berry (2008: 111):

> This work on resistance in some form is probably at the base of all the work, for it makes us realise that any form of communication, however off-beat or minimal, is a way of reaching out to some other person and affirming one's presence in some way – and yet you can be 'cool' at the same time: but most important, it makes us realise that words always cost something.

I realized with Butterfly how this resistance physicalizes the Stakes in responding to another person's behaviour. The resistance triggers the body's efforts in the struggle to be free. This is then reflected in the actor's vocal expression and makes it clear how much the words cost. This next exercise allows you to discover in the moment with your partner how much you now want and *need* the heightened nature of the text because it matches the expression that you are feeling, engendered by your conditions, in response to the other actors. Now only the words and how you use them are at your disposal to get what you want.

1   Actors stand behind the back of their chairs about two metres apart and facing each other. Check the chairs are high enough so you can stand comfortably and rest your hands on the backs of them. You might need to stack a few chairs for tall people.

2   Actors connect to their Five Conditions for the scene. To do this you can walk away from your chairs, doing whatever you need to do, moving freely to get into your Prep. When ready, stand in place behind your chair, looking down.

3   When both actors are ready, look up and take a moment to connect with each other. From now on, you cannot move at all apart from your eyes and mouths.

4   Begin the scene, speaking each word more slowly than usual in order to discover what each word itself has to offer.

5   At all times you should be thinking: 'Is it working?' (The director can also prompt this at any time.) You can look at each other or choose not to look, whichever helps you get your Objective.

6   You need to have relaxed hands resting on the tops of the chair backs at all times. Directors should watch for tension creeping in or actors gripping the chairs. Encourage them to soften their knees.

7   Directors should also watch out for heads jutting forward. You can touch the back of their heads gently to remind them to relax and not poke their heads forward in a chicken pose.

Reasons to do the exercise

• It allows actors to reach emotional places that might be out of their comfort zone. The very act of saying these words in this way heightens people's passions, playfulness and aggression. It gives them permission to be even more unjust, charming, sensual or unpleasant.

• It is very useful for characters who do not have much text in scenes to really see how and when they have an impulse to speak.

- The speaking of the words empowers your sense of Entitlement. By allowing you to say things out loud it makes them more truthful, which helps you commit to the words more.

- Actors can easily undermine the expressive power of the words through physical distractions. If they cannot move, they learn to harness rather than diffuse the power of their text.

Example: *Romeo and Juliet* (3.5)

Lord Capulet's tirade against Juliet and in turn his wife and the Nurse in *Romeo and Juliet* (3.5.141–68) needs a lot of commitment to release more aggressive feelings. He's just found out that Juliet is refusing to marry Paris, the most eligible man of the town that he has arranged for her to marry. When this exercise is done behind the chairs, it releases the actor playing Lord Capulet into finding all the colours of rage and not just playing angry on one note. They really discover the ugliness needed; all the disgust, the hurt, betrayal, the nastiness, shaming and humiliating language now are released through the words while their body is restricted. Meanwhile, everyone feels entirely safe as, stuck behind chairs, it is only through speaking the words and exploring the impulses to speak that the violence in the language is used.

Since Meisner is all about 'living off the other fellow', how useful are his techniques for soliloquies?

Meisner's principles still apply but instead of responding to your fellow actors, you are responding to the audience. In soliloquies you need to really see the audience clearly and really respond to them. Actors can be concerned that they will be 'put off' by the audience and so train themselves (and indeed are often trained) not to let the audience affect them. Directly addressing the audience is easier in shared light, such as in immersive productions or outdoor theatres, but even in the dark you can sense the audience. If you have an 'As If' on them and treat them as another character, and if you are *really* trying get them to do something, then everything they do becomes a goldmine of things you can see clearly and respond to honestly: their attentiveness, their folded arms, their looks away, their discomfort, their boredom, their smiles, their giggles and particularly the response they will mainly give you, their silence. Ask yourself, what is the quality of this silence, how do you perceive it from the point of view of your character? Are they agreeing with you? Are they too ashamed or hurt to answer you? Do you take it as tacit approval, or as disapproval? When Helena says in *A Midsummer Night's Dream* (1.1.246–51):

> I will go tell him of fair Hermia's flight:
> Then to the wood will he, tomorrow night,
> Pursue her; and for this intelligence
> If I have thanks, it is a dear expense.
> But herein mean I to enrich my pain,
> To have his sight thither and back again.

. . . Well, no one told her not to. Not only do we see what we want to see; in an audience's silence, characters hear what they want to hear.

Useful Objectives on the audience in soliloquies are:

- Get them to be on my side . . .
- Get them to trust me . . .
- Get them to agree with me . . .

Useful 'As Ifs' on the audience in soliloquies are:

- People who should be on my side
- People who are not on my side
- People who judge me unfairly
- People who are my confidantes

Example: *Macbeth* (3.1.47–50)

Straight after Macbeth has spoken to the murderers to arrange the killing of Banquo, he turns to the audience, who he knows have witnessed not only that secretive plot but the whole events of the play so far. His Objective could be: 'Get them to nod in agreement with me because if they do that means they support me in getting rid of the person who knows my secrets ...' He senses the audience are condemning him with their silent stares and so in his unspoken inner monologue, he immediately justifies himself: *What are you staring at me for? Don't look at me like that.* Aloud he says: 'To be thus is nothing'. His inner voice continues, *Oh you've got nothing to say? Why are you frowning? I'll explain further.* He speaks: 'But to be safely thus'. His inner voice asks: *Don't you agree? Silence? I'll spell it out for you.* His speech goes on: 'Our fears in Banquo / Stick deep'. He looks at the audience, thinking, *You know why* and continues speaking: 'and in his royalty of nature / Reigns that which would be fear'd'. *Surely you must understand now,* he thinks. *You heard the prophecy. Don't you agree? No? No one? Don't you look away from me ...*

As Macbeth, you are considering what body language, eye contact, facial expressions, sounds and words you are looking for from *everyone* in the audience to know if it's going well and you are getting your Objective. If you haven't got their full agreement by the end of the speech, you know you will have to show them they are wrong. Asides work in the same way as soliloquies, as the actor is simply treating the audience as another character and has Five Conditions for that 'dialogue', getting the audience emotionally involved in the journey.

When we performed a production of *Macbeth* in Poole's Cavern in Buxton the audience were surrounding Nick Danan, a very experienced actor, who had drawn them into a dark bit of the cave, having happily waved Banquo and Fleance on their way and got rid of Lady Macbeth. He turned to the audience and got them, all of them, as they stood amongst dripping stalactites in the flickering candlelight, to nod in agreement with him. We got a review that said, 'I woke up this morning very unsettled as I felt I had encouraged Macbeth to kill Banquo.'

Summary of Butterfly's techniques for working on text

Learning lines uninflected and 'beyond learning' brings immense freedom in being able to respond in the moment. Paraphrasing the text into words you would personally say brings deep ownership and connection. Adapting Meisner's exercise of 'Breaking the Back' as a rehearsal technique of speaking the lines under the Five Conditions breaks the habit of inflected patterns and avoids speaking in a 'Shakespeare voice'. Speaking the lines 'Back to Back' develops the skills of listening actively and being affected by your partner's words. 'Using the Words to get your Objective' develops Cicely Berry's displacement exercises into a rehearsal technique that makes actors work hard to use their words in the most effective ways. By shutting down physical impulses, the voice has to express itself more fully. For soliloquies and asides, always ensure you have an Objective on the audience as another character. This allows you to respond to the audience as you would any other character, responding to their behaviour in terms of whether it helps or hinders you in achieving your Objective.

REFERENCES

Adler, S. (2000), *The Art of Acting*, ed. H. Kissel. New York: Applause.

Ball, W. (1994), *A Sense of Direction: Some Observations on the Art of Directing*, London: Quite Specific Media.

Barton, J. (1984), *Playing Shakespeare*, London, Methuen Drama.

Bernardin, M. (2020), interview conducted by the authors via Zoom on 6 May 2020.

Berry, C. (1987), *The Actor and His Text*, London: Harrap.

Berry, C. (2001), *Text in Action. A Definitive Guide to Exploring Text in Rehearsal for Actors and Directors*, London: Virgin.

Berry, C. (2004), *Working Shakespeare. The Cicely Berry Workshops*, The Working Arts Library.

Berry, C. (2008), *From Word to Play. A Handbook for Directors*. London: Oberon.

Bruder, M. et al. (1986), *A Practical Handbook for the Actor*, New York: Vintage.

Carnicke, S.M. (2008), *Stanislavsky in Focus for the Twenty-first Century*. London: Routledge.

Clurman, H. (1975), *The Fervent Years: The Group Theatre and the 30s*, New York: Da Capo Press.

Crystal, D. and B. Crystal (2002), *Shakespeare's Words: A Glossary and Language Companion*, London: Penguin.

Esper, W. and D. DiMarco (2008), *The Actor's Art and Craft: William Esper Teaches the Meisner Technique*, New York: Anchor.

Esper, W. and D. DiMarco (2014), *The Actor's Guide to Creating a Character: William Esper Teaches the Meisner Technique*, New York: Anchor.

Ewan, V. and K. Sagovsky (2018), *Laban Efforts in Action: A Movement Handbook for Actors with Online Video Resources*, London: Bloomsbury.

Hagen, U. (1973), *Respect for Acting*, New Jersey: Wiley.

Kahneman, D. (2012), *Thinking Fast and Slow*, London: Penguin.

Lee Strasberg Theatre and Film Institute (n.d.). Available online: https://strasberg.edu/about (accessed 15 November 2019).

Mamet, D. (1998), *True and False: Heresy and Common Sense for the Actor*, London: Bloomsbury.

Mehrabian, A. (1972), *Silent Messages: Implicit Communication of Emotions and Attitudes*, Belmont, CA: Wadsworth.

Meisner, S. and D. Longwell (1987), *Sanford Meisner on Acting*, New York: Vintage.

Miller, A. (2000), *The Collected Essays of Arthur Miller*, London: Bloomsbury.

Neighborhood Playhouse (n.d.). Available online: http://neighborhoodplayhouse.org/home (accessed 6 May 2020).

Ney, C. (2016), *Directing Shakespeare in America: Current Practices*, London: Bloomsbury.

Rippon, G. (2019), *The Gendered Brain. The New Neuroscience that Shatters the Myth of the Female Brain*, London: Vintage.

Ryan, A. (2020), interview conducted by the authors in Margate on 15 January 2020.

Sanford Meisner Centre (n.d.), 'Our Tradition'. Available online: https://www.themeisnercenter.com/classes.html (accessed 6 May 2020).

Shirley, D. (2010), '"The Reality of Doing": Meisner Technique and British Actor Training', *Theatre, Dance and Performance Training*, 1:2, 199–213.

Stanislavski, C. (1981), *Creating a Role*, London: Methuen.

Strandberg-Long, P. (2018), 'Mapping Meisner – How Stanislavski's System Influenced Meisner's Process and Why it Matters to British Drama School Training Today', *Stanislavski Studies*, 6:1, 11–19.

Trimble, M. (2012), *Why Humans Like to Cry: Tragedy, Evolution and the Brain*, Oxford: OUP.

Wilkinson, R. and K. Pickett (2009), *The Spirit Level: Why Equality is Better for Everyone*, London: Allen Lane.

Williams, S. (2020), interview conducted by the authors in London on 11 January 2020.

ABOUT THE AUTHORS

Aileen Gonsalves works professionally as a theatre practitioner: acting, writing and directing across all mediums. She is Artistic Director of Butterfly Theatre Company, which specializes in immersive theatre in extraordinary locations around Europe. The company uses her pioneering actor training approach, the Gonsalves Method, which is rooted in Meisner. Aileen teaches across many drama schools and companies internationally, including as Head of the MA in Acting at Arts Ed (2011–15) and Head of BA Acting at Drama Studio London (2018–19). Her expertise is in authentic acting and directing, particularly with Shakespeare and Meisner. She has worked extensively with the RSC as an actor, director and education associate practitioner. She is an associate artist with Kali Theatre Company developing UK women writers of South Asian heritage. She is founding the UK's first Immersive Acting School using her Gonsalves Method and is developing online courses (along with Tracy) for using acting approaches in the teaching of Shakespeare.

Tracy Irish is an education practitioner, writer, researcher and teacher with a specialism in Shakespeare. She has been a core member of the RSC's education team since their innovative 'Stand Up for Shakespeare' Campaign in 2008 and also works regularly with the University of Birmingham and the University of Warwick. Her particular interest is in developing communication skills through theatre-based approaches. As the Warwick Business School Shakespeare Scholar, she completed an interdisciplinary PhD on the value of theatre-based approaches for teaching Shakespeare, which was influenced by her previous role leading the RSC's international education project for the 2012 World Shakespeare Festival. She has authored a range of articles and resources including 'Theatre, Education and Embodied Cognition' in *The Palgrave Handbook of Women on Stage, RSC School Shakespeare* editions and the online *Shakespeare Learning Zone*.